MONEY MAKING
secrets of the
MILLIONAIRES

MONEY MAKING
secrets of the
MILLIONAIRES

Hal D. Steward

PARKER PUBLISHING COMPANY, INC.

West Nyack, N.Y.

© 1972 By

PARKER PUBLISHING COMPANY, INC.

West Nyack, N.Y.

Library of Congress
Catalog Card Number: 70-182500

Printed in the United States of America

ISBN 0-13-600320-6

B&P

A Word from the Author

You're the main character in this book. It's been researched and written with one purpose only: To make you more successful than you are presently. And to accomplish this, I've made you, the reader, the focus—the main character.

It was Thomas Carlyle who said, "All that Mankind has done, thought, gained or been is lying as in magic preservation in the pages of Books. They are the chosen possession of men."

In this book, then, are explored and preserved the secrets of men who've achieved outstanding success. All you have to do to learn them, is to read this book.

Through study, reading, I've seen miracles happen to men and women in all walks of life all over the world. Miracles will happen to you, too, when you begin to apply the power you'll gain from the use of the techniques revealed in this book. It'll teach you how to achieve the kind of success you've always sought.

This book, I believe, may be your magic "money magnet" because as Aldous Huxley said, "Every man who knows how to read has it in his power to magnify himself, to multiply the ways in which he exists, to make his life full, significant and interesting."

9

Let me say now, at the beginning, you'll find nothing difficult in these pages; the methods and techniques described are proven ones—every one of them has been tried and used to gain success. And they all worked quickly and easily, in many cases practically without effort.

You'll learn in these pages why one man is sad and another man happy. Why one is joyful and prosperous and another man poor and miserable. Why fear and anxiety has permeated the life of one man while another man is full of belief in himself and has self-confidence.

You'll learn why one man is a great success and another a dismal failure. Why some men achieve personal satisfaction, wealth, and happiness in their profession or occupation while other men toil and fret all their lives without doing or accomplishing anything worthwhile.

And you'll learn why one woman has made a happy, successful marriage, while another knows only heartache, failure, and rejection.

Why the difference between the successes and the failures? That's what this book is all about.

My reason for writing it has been to answer and clarify the above questions and many others like them. I've tried to explain what my research has disclosed to be the great fundamental truths about human success and failure; and I believe I've achieved my objective.

I urge you to study this book and apply the wealth secrets revealed herein; and if you do, I am convinced that you will have the means to radically change your life for the better. It'll lift you from the ranks of the losers; it'll put you out of confusion, misery, melancholy, and failure. It'll guide you to a life of happiness, personal satisfaction, achievement, comfort, and success.

So, I suggest you read this book carefully, earnestly, repeatedly, and lovingly. Prove to yourself the amazing, fantastic way it can help you. It could be, and I believe it will be, the turning point in your life.

I've attempted in writing this book to give it a unique feature—practicality. Here you are presented with simple, usable techniques and methods which you can easily apply in your own life and work. You'll find the book packed with case studies of men and women who've actually used them to reap wealth beyond their wildest dreams, to leap from poverty to plenty overnight, to make thousands of dollars of extra income virtually without work from businesses that practically run themselves—to achieve unusual, incredible success.

Everyone desires happiness, personal achievement, and wealth, but many don't know how to go about getting them. This book tells you how. All you have to do is study it, adopt the methods and techniques described, and then use them as your own.

When you do you'll suddenly find you're confronted with a new, purposeful, useful, and prosperous life. Can you ask for more?

Hal D. Steward

Contents

MONEY MAKING
secrets of the
MILLIONAIRES

MILLIONAIRE SECRET #1

How to Magnetize the Money Power within You

Let's begin with the acceptance of an essential point: You can control your destiny—if you magnetize the money power within you. I intend to show you how. I won't ask you to daydream, or to engage in somewhere in never-never land. The fact that you can control your destiny is the solid rock foundation on which I'll show you how to build your own personal and business or professional success.

You can control what you do and where you do it. Ponder that. What does it mean? It simply means that if you don't like your present job, you don't have to stick it out. If you don't like the neighborhood you live in, you don't have to live there. If you don't want to struggle to make ends meet, you can earn more money. You're where you are because you've accepted things as they are. You can change all that as soon as you change your thoughts and then support them with action.

These are the conclusions I've drawn after years of study and research into the subject of what makes a person a success. This book is the distillation of what I've learned from interviews with successful men the world over. When I began my project I set out to determine what essential elements separate men of success from those of failure. What you'll read here is the result.

Granted, the thesis of this book is new and different from that contained in many of the so-called "success" books. It's different in that it offers you a practical, workable method of achieving success rather than a theory that is simply more or less academic.

Throughout this book I'm going to be discussing with you Desire and Action. Those are the key elements to the psychology of self-achievement. One doesn't work without the other. So, right now implant in your mind those two words: Desire and Action. I'm going to show you through my own experience and the experiences of other successful men how you can use them to achieve the ultimate of your dreams quickly and easily, practically without effort.

If you're realistic and haven't yet achieved the success you believe yourself capable of, you know it's because you've let others control your destiny. They've decided where you live, what job you hold, how much you earn. Who are "they"? Why they're your parents, your wife, your boss, your friends, your teachers, and others you haven't even met yet.

Without being aware of it, you may have turned your destiny over to them. You may have, for all practical purposes, abrogated your destiny, your future to their desires and their actions instead of your own.

You don't have to be such a victim. You don't have to accept things as they are. You have the power to choose. The choice you make, the decision that is yours, should be directly related to your own goals, not someone else's. When you're after success, choose what you consider best for yourself without regards to the self-interest opinions of others. Until you do you won't achieve success, nor will you be entitled to it.

Until you make a positive move in the direction of the things you want most, you'll attract nothing worthwhile. Minus decision, you cannot properly magnetize the money power within you. An unsettled mind attracts only unsettled conditions.

But let no one, me included, delude you that thoughts alone will achieve success for you. They won't. They are the key to your success only when combined with action.

Louis Pasteur, for instance, could have thought all his life about how he'd like to discover a serum to prevent rabies. But without action, in his case, laboratory experiments, he'd never have developed the Pasteur Treatment.

Victor Hugo wrote, "No army can withstand the strength of an idea whose time has come." I believe he's right. But without action, no idea can be executed into reality.

Let's now, briefly, look at the character, the make-up, of a failure, a loser. He's the fellow who's able to endure his dull, routine job without either making a wholehearted commitment to it or questioning it so severely that he becomes bound in conscience to reject it. Why doesn't he have an appetite for searching out or creating a new job? He has, in effect, accepted his failure; he's let others make his decisions for him. He, then, has made a deal with his failure; he indulges it. The failure has become a prisoner of his lack of desire and action; he's a hostage of inertia. He's inclined to suppose that there must be better, more rewarding jobs, ones that are more exhilarating, but he dismisses them as being out of his reach, as unattainable by him.

The failure, then, isn't really a truly alive, ambitious, functioning person; he's, in fact, simply functioning as a human echo. He hasn't grasped, analyzed, and criticised for his existence, until he's given himself a logical explanation for his failure, until he's assimilated unto himself those desires, those thoughts, and those plans for action that'll change his life and lead him onto the path of success.

What I'm saying is that when a person has arrived at the point where he accepts failure without combat, then he's ready to accept almost any shabby substitute that will free him from having to resist. When this happens he can no longer experience the summit of happiness, nor can he ever have a cultivated mind.

"A cultivated mind," wrote the English philospher, John Stuart Mills, "finds sources of inexhaustible interest in all that surrounds it; in the objects of nature, the achievements of art, the imagination of poetry, the incidents of history, the ways of mankind, past and present, and their prospects in the future."

The successful man, or woman. has sought to develop a cultivated mind. In his search and acquisition of knowledge he's prepared himself for success.

How, you ask, do you begin to cultivate your own mind? There are, I believe, three basic steps:

1. You think success to achieve success; that is, you imagine yourself to be what you plan to become. You recognize that action begins with thought; that organized mind-power is the greatest power in the world.

2. You self-discipline yourself. Either by self-education or by going to college you discipline yourself to study every day of your life. You set out to become an authority on one particular subject with the objective of knowing more about that subject than any other person in the world.

3. You act. You do this by using your acquired knowledge to enter a new profession or business, to improve your personal life, to earn more money or to achieve whatever other goal you've set for yourself.

Let me here, though, offer a caution: When you think of success you decide the direction of your thoughts; don't let someone else decide it for you. You can stop thinking about useless things. You can substitute positive, active, success-bearing thoughts. The more thinking hours you devote to positive thoughts of success, the quicker you'll begin to magnetize the money power within you, and achieve your goals.

Now let me return to my basic thesis that "desire" and "action" are the two major elements of success. If you accept this, then you also accept the fact that life is change. You know the smallest disturbance alters the pattern of the whole. The environment changes, and man with it. It's up to you to have an influence over your own environment and to control your destiny as the changes occur.

Movement, healthy conflict, is the motivating factor of achievement. Action is what counts. Every manifestation of life is action.

Let's look at it another way: Our ancestor, the cave man, killed that he might eat—that was certainly action.

But twentieth century man, for the most part, creates action a different way. If, for instance, he wants success, he acts by preparing himself through study, observation, and application.

For a moment, let's imagine you're Henry J. Kaiser, the man who built all those ships in World War II. You'd use his success secret, which simply put by him is: "Know yourself and decide what you want most of all to make out of your life. Then write down your goals and plan to reach them."

That's precisely what Kaiser did and this "money magnet" technique propelled him into the ranks of the millionaires. It worked for him, why shouldn't it work for you?

As you know, everything comes from something else; action cannot come of itself. Look at it this way: When you state a proposition, a goal, that is called a thesis. Then the reasons why you can't achieve your goal are called antithesis. You then form a third proposition, the synthesis, being the combination of the original proposition and the contradiction to it.

These three steps—thesis, antithesis, and synthesis—are the law of all movement, all action. Everything that moves constantly negates itself. All things change toward their opposite through movement. The present becomes the past, the future becomes the present. There isn't anything which doesn't move.

You and I, therefore, are a maze of seeming contradictions. We plan one thing, then at once we do another; how can we explain these contradictions? How can we use the law of movement to achieve our goals?

Let's assume, to make the point, that you're a gentle, inoffensive man, who's never hurt anyone, never broken the law, but nevertheless you have a dull, routine job that offers you no future or opportunity for real success. Suddenly, one Sunday while you're out pleasure driving with your wife you see a beautiful house for sale. You stop and you and your wife go inside and inspect it.

On your return home you look around at your own drab surroundings, a small two bedroom apartment in a low-rent district. Under your critical eyes it sheds all the requirements you think necessary for an adequate home. For one thing, you decide it's old; for another, it looks cheap and shabby. Your wife isn't blind; you know she always is aware of her near-poverty existence.

You decide you must have a new home; a large, costly one. But how? You have no money. What you earn barely supports you and your wife. No, you can't buy a new home.

For the first time you feel old. You know you're over 30, that it'll be years, if ever, before you can even save enough money to make the down payment on the type of home you want to live in. What's the use of planning—of living—of attempting to give yourself and your wife a hope for a brighter, more comfortable future? Nothing can come of it, anyway. So you push back in your mind your desire for a new home.

This step, pushing your desire back in your mind, makes you cross at home, listless in your job. You brood over your situation, you're despondent. Despite your efforts to do so, you can't stop thinking about that beautiful house you inspected. You begin to wonder what your wife thinks of you? Has she lost respect for you because you can't give her the things you know she'd like to have? You become less and less productive in your job. This doesn't improve your disposition.

Now because of your despondency, you make a decision. You go on a frantic hunt for a better job that'll pay you more money and offer you greater opportunity. You find nothing after a drawn-out, fruitless search. You feel even more useless than before.

All this, you see, is conflict—movement. Like almost all conflict it can be traced to your environment, the social conditions under which you live.

You have reached a crisis in your life. The way you go next may modify your future for either better or worse.

Now the question arises: Of what are you made? How determined are you? How much stamina have you? What amount of disappointment, discouragement and suffering can you endure? What is your hope for the future? How farseeing are you? Have you imagination? Have you the ability to plan a long-range program for yourself and the self-discipline necessary to stick to it?

If you are sufficiently aroused—if you have an urgent, overpowering desire—you'll make a decision. And this decision will set into motion forces to counteract whatever opposes you. If, for instance, lack of education is one of the opposing forces, you'll combat it by better educating yourself. Should your fear of taking a risk oppose you, you'll mentally condition yourself to take well thought out, calculated risks.

On the other hand, if you make a decision, but lack the mental strength to see it through, you'll fail. You'll be unwilling to do those things required to achieve your goal; you'll join the permanent ranks of the losers. And if you haven't the persistence, the determination, to achieve your objectives that's where you belong, among the failures.

So, again we are back to my original point: It takes desire and action persistently applied to achieve success.

In my preparation to write this book, I interviewed countless successful men in a variety of fields. I attempted through these interviews and other research to put my finger on the one quality or qualities these men possessed in common. When I was finished, I found, without exception, that the one quality that set all these men apart from their less-successful colleagues was determination That was their most jealously-guarded "money secret"!

That's right, determination. I was convinced, after interviewing these men, that their determination to succeed—to be successful in every possible way—was the prime reason they'd obtained their goals. Their inflexible desire to succeed enabled them to do it.

Okay, you say, so far you've discussed setting goals and achieving them through desire and action. But, now you ask, how do I know what decisions to make to achieve my goal and whether they're the proper ones?

Decisions can, I know, be a problem. Just think of the hundreds of small decisions you make in your everyday life. Most of them are routine; others have a direct effect upon your future.

The successful man is by make-up a decision-maker. Uncertainty is his opponent. Overcoming it is his mission. Whether the outcome is a consequence of luck or of wisdom, the moment of decision is without doubt the most creative and critical event in the life of the successful man.

Let's define a decision; It's choice of alternative means by which to move forward to an objective. The objective itself may involve a complex of desires—that is, it may be a combination of objectives some of which are in conflict. Your ultimate goal, for instance, may conflict with your present job.

If you approach your decision-making in an orderly way, you'll arrive at your decision in five steps: (1) You'll determine your objective; (2) You'll pull together all available information on the situation that confronts you and determine the courses of action you have; (3) Now you analyze the opposing courses of action to your objective; (4) You compare your own courses of action against each other; and, finally, (5) You make your decision.

As a decision-maker you, in effect, stand between past events and future events. Successful men, in a surprising number of cases, believe the outcome of their decisions is a certainty. You should develop the same attitude; don't become a victim of indecision.

There's a way, however, to cure the problem of indecisiveness if it affects you. That is, take a hint from the successful man. Notice how he talks. Watch him in action. One thing stands out immediately: He makes up his mind fast. His instructions are crisp and to the point. What's his secret? Simply put: He knows what he wants. He has a goal. Experience has taught him a basic lesson: You stop wandering all over the lot when you know where you're going.

The successful man, then, never loses sight of his goal. It's anchored in his brain. Therefore, when he's faced with a decision, he asks himself: "What should my decision be to move me along faster toward my goal?"

It works, so try it.

Now, you ask, how do I go about choosing a goal? That's a personal desire only you can answer. What do you want to achieve? Do you want a better job, more money, or do you want to live a life different from your present one? Establish your goal, then visualize it. Once you've done this then set intermediate steps along the way toward your achieving it.

There is, however, still one further element in what I call the "success pattern"—the psychology of self-achievement. It's having a good self-image.

You know, for instance, that a person who has a good self-image enjoys a kind of peace, because he's focused in on others, on events, on ideas, on activities outside himself. He takes himself for what he is, based on a deep belief in himself. He's not smug, he's realistic. In short, he has a kind of quiet conviction that he can meet the threats and pressing necessities of life.

If you have a good self-image you'll find, for example, that you'll be able to make decisions without fear of being wrong. You'll also discover you'll get along better with others. The person with a good self-image knows that in the course of his development he's exposed to a variety of pressures from his environment and he learns how to adjust or adapt himself to these pressures.

So, since you behave in a social environment you're also exposed to the reactions of others and, by implication, their reaction to your behavior. Their evaluations serve as a "feedback" on the basis of which you not only may alter your behavior or reinforce it, but also develop a picture of yourself. The point is: If you act like a success, others will evaluate you as a success.

A good self-image, then is a man's adequate conception of himself. He doesn't have to be a social lion, nor deliriously happy or over-optimistic. All he has to be is himself. And he knows he may not always be successful, but he also knows he isn't a failure. He's capable of love and understanding.

How, then, do you improve your self-image if you believe it isn't what it should be?

The first step, obviously, is to recognize that a change in your self-image is needed. A good sign it needs a change is when you project what you think of yourself, particularly to justify failure, onto others. When, for instance, you fall victim to the unhappy belief that nobody gives you a chance, what you actually should recognize is that you don't give yourself a chance.

Then, as a second step, you can begin to change your self-image simply by doing things for others. The easiest way is to recognize the importance of others by helping them and letting them help you.

This is how you learn to enjoy others, get along with them, and eventually charm them. As you improve your attitude toward people, something bounces off which helps your self-evaluation.

As a third step, it's important to feel that you do a job well enough to feel some pride of effort and accomplishment.

The improvement of yourself physically is the fourth step toward an improved self-image. Get in good shape. Walk, swim, exercise, do whatever is necessary to better your health.

And, fifth, maintain and increase your ability to enjoy yourself. Enjoying life improves your self-image. As one psychologist has said:

> If we do not maintain a certain level of pleasure, we get irritable and hostile and depressed, and soon we get discouraged, and all this feeds self-rejection. There are pleasures available to everyone. They may be small, but they count, too . . . But most of all, the enjoyment of people is worth re-emphasis. The lonely, socially fearful person is not telling himself the truth when he says he enjoys life best when he is left alone. He wants people and wants them to want him. He simply has not yet learned the technique of reaching out.

Let's now, again, return to the subject of magnetizing your money power—another name for which is goal setting. What guide can you use to help you set your personal and attainable goal? For assistance use this checklist:

1. Establish your goal based upon an all-powerful, overriding personal desire. Set as your goal the income you want to achieve in a certain period of time, or the job you ultimately want, or where and how you'd like to live. Decide and set for your goal, for instance, what you want to accomplish in the next 10 years. When you reach that goal, you then can set an even higher one.

2. Set intermediate goals but don't tie yourself down to a strict timetable on them. If, for example, you're 30 years old and your goal is to earn $25,000 a year by age 40, set intermediate goals of increasing your earnings so much each year. You'll have a constant feeling of achievement as you meet and gain these lesser goals along the way. But if you fall short of your intermediate goals occasionally, don't get discouraged. Redirect your energy to get back on the track.

3. Concentrate on current efforts. Although you must keep your ultimate goal in mind, do your best in your present job.

That's the best way to guarantee your reaching your big goal.

4. Don't permit roadblocks to detour you. Your intermediate, short-range goals may not always work out. When they fall short, don't let it bother you. Pick up whatever you can and move on. Decide what your best move will be to continue toward your major goal. Once you've made your decision, don't look back, don't get into the "If-I'd-only-done-so-and-so" frame of mind—it's self-defeating. Learn by your errors along the way and avoid repeating them.

5. Avoid impulsive, ill-considered, decisions. If you're faced with a major decision, study the problem, analyze it from every viewpoint, allow it to simmer for a while in your subconcious mind, then apply the best knowledge and information you have to its solution.

6. Don't fret about future decisions. Avoid potential problems that may never develop. You know that most worrying is done about things that never occur. So, face each decision as it comes; not those that may or may not confront you in the indefinite future.

7. Adopt a self-image improvement program. Learn to have confidence and belief in yourself. Don't worry about being wrong, and if disappointment comes face it squarely and courageously. If you have to, change your strategy, but never take your sights off your ultimate goal.

Someone once said, "Don't take your eyes off the stars, but never lose sight of the streetlamps." Put another way, have a big dream, a large goal, but don't lose touch with the practical steps you must take along the way to achieve your life's ambition.

A final word of advice: When you set your sights on the future, and establish your goal, then raise it to twice the height you believe you can reach. It'll be closer to your real worth than you realize.

Then remember what I said at the beginning of this chapter: You can control your own destiny, but to do so you must have a strong desire and be anxious to take the action needed to achieve what you want for yourself and those you love.

MILLIONAIRE SECRET #2

How to Convert Wishes into Reality

When James Joseph Ling was in his early twenties, and in the U.S. Navy, he decided he wanted to become a licensed electrical engineer—his desire to do so was all-powerful. So he read and memorized two books: *The Electrical Engineers Handbook* and *The National Electrical Code.* The contents of these books, plus information gleaned from a borrowed correspondence course text, enabled him to pass the city of Dallas electrical engineering exam on the second try. He was 22 at the time.

Ling today is the Ling in the Ling-Temco-Vought Corporation and one of America's richest men. He's only 46.

But in 1946, when he passed the electrical engineering exam, he was a high school dropout with four years in the Navy behind him. And once he'd passed the exam he didn't want to become someone's employee. His urge, his desire, was to control his own destiny.

"I wanted to get into the electrical contracting business," he says, "but I didn't want to wait 10 to 12 years, which was the fashion at that time. I remember that I applied for a job at Dallas Power and Light. They took me to a large room and showed me the competition—about 250 guys my age or older, some of them much older, bending over drafting boards. I saw

35

that wasn't what I had in mind. Also, the salary, about $175 a month, didn't appeal to me."

So, with a meager stake of $3,000 Ling opened his own contracting business. Twenty years later he headed his own corporation that ranked 38th among the largest companies in the nation with annual sales of $1.8 billion.

What were the elements of Ling's success?

First, it was, as he admits, the desire to succeed, and succeed rapidly.

Second, his staying power. "It's the staying power that makes the difference between winners and losers," he said.

Ling's goal is to become the nation's most powerful man as well as its richest. Already he's one of the richest. He owns a $2 million Dallas mansion, a fleet of jets he personally pilots to European money capitals; an envied art collection and about 17 percent of the 38th largest corporation in the country.

The point I'm making here, using Ling as an example, is that nothing can stymie a man with the desire, the determination, to succeed. Your success is assured just as surely as the sun rises in in the morning.

Jim Ling is a man who knows he controls his own destiny. If he has a secret to his success, it's this: If you really want something badly enough, it'll happen because you make it happen. But it will happen only if you're willing to do something about it—plan, work at it, and work at it hard.

Desire, then, to want something badly, is the first essential key to success. I don't mean though simply to wish for something. That's unrealistic. Until now, perhaps it has seemed impossible for you to miraculously convert wishes into reality But there is a magic power that can do just that—the driving force of a burning desire to succeed.

The difference, then, between desire and wishing is one of intensity. Wishing is undernourished wanting. It's for the losers. It doesn't have the power to propel you to success. Desire is the high-power ingredient you need.

But, you ask, how do I build a strong desire to succeed?—How *do* I convert wishes into reality?

As a first step, simply take a sheet of paper and list those things you'd like to achieve within the next six months or one year. The list will help clarify your thinking. When you have it completed, you'll notice that some of the objectives on it may not be attainable for five or 10 years—cross them off, stick just to those you believe you can achieve within the next six months or one year.

Now, as the second step; choose the objective on the list you desire most. That's your goal for achievement within the next six months or one year, whichever time length you've decided.

From the moment you select your goal—the objective you've decided you most desire—it should never be out of your thoughts until you achieve it. Memorize it, think about it constantly, consider it whenever you're faced with either a personal or a career decision.

Let me give you a warning: Don't entertain negative thoughts about your goal. That is, don't say, "I want it but I know I'll never obtain it in such a short period of time because of so-and-so." If a negative thought enters your brain, force it out, quickly, with a positive thought.

And do this: Write out your goal on a card and paste it on the bathroom mirror where you shave, tape down another copy of it on the night table beside your bed, afix it to your office desk top, and have it listed on the book mark you use when reading. Keep it always before you.

Now I'm assuming you've arrived at your desire, your goal, in a realistic way. That is, you haven't decided you're going to become an attorney-at-law in the next six months or year when you have only a high school education. If that's your ultimate goal, your big one, then your six months or one year goal should be something like this: "I will earn at least 15 college semester units by January 1, 197— as part of the academic requirement to enter Law School."

You ask, why is an all-consuming desire an essential aid to success? Simply because your success is a direct result of your effort to achieve it—physical as well as mental effort. Your effort can only be motivated by a strong desire.

You realize, of course, that when I suggest a goal to be obtained within the six months or one year, I'm discussing an intermediate goal. It is a goal or goals you'll set for yourself along the path to achievement of your major, your ultimate, life's goal.

Let me give you an example from my own personal life. My ultimate, or major, goal, the one I'd set as my life's ambition, was to support myself totally by writing books. But to learn to write more effectively I decided that one of my intermediate goals should be to obtain a job on a metropolitan newspaper as a reporter so I could learn by experience, and the guidance of the editors, how to write better. At the time I was comfortably established in Boston. My future could have been secure as a college teacher; but I wanted to write books.

So, I threw over everything and drove across the country to Los Angeles where I wanted to live while I worked as a reporter. I had no idea whether I'd be able to land a job as a reporter, but I'd decided the risk was important. I would succeed or fail, but I'd take the risk.

I succeeded.

How did I do it?

Once in Los Angeles, I walked into the City Room of the Los Angeles *Examiner,* and introduced myself to Frederick B. Kinne, the City Editor. I told him I wanted a job as a general assignment reporter. After I'd given him a brief sketch of my background, Kinne picked up a sheet of paper containing some facts and asked me to turn them into a news story.

I did as I was instructed. When I'd finished the story, he read it and said, "When can you be ready to go to work?"

"Right now," I answered.

Later Fred Kinne told me that if I'd answered that last question in any other way he wouldn't have hired me. But, he said, my determination to get a job and succeed at it was evident in my willingness to take off my coat and go immediately to work.

Not long afterward, the *Examiner* suspended publication. Fred Kinne was appointed assistant managing editor of *The San Diego Union* and asked me to work on that newspaper. I was delighted and went to work for him as a general assignment reporter.

Fred Kinne, who today is editor of the San Diego *Evening Tribune,* gave me my chance. And I did my best to prove to him he hadn't made a mistake in judgment when he hired me.

But I had on my own time, after working hours, prepared myself for a metropolitan newspaper job.

First, I'd taken a correspondence course in journalism from the Newspaper Institute of America in New York. I'd studied every book on journalism I could find. For years before I arrived in Los Angeles I'd written newspaper and magazine freelance articles. I had also decided I must learn as much as I could about business, management, and law, so I completed correspondence courses from LaSalle Extension University, Chicago, and the Alexander Hamilton Institute, New York.

So, you see, if modesty permits, I'd prepared myself for the job Fred Kinne offered me.

And I've told you precisely how I did it.

My point is that each person who succeeds, who wins, in any undertaking must be willing to burn his bridges behind him and cut off all his sources of retreat. Only by so doing can he be sure of maintaining that state of mind known as a burning, unquenchable, desire to win; the first essential to success.

How strong does your desire have to be?

Let's look at the case of George Stanley, who in 1957 was the owner-operator of a cold storage plant in Indiana. He was 48 years old, had less than a high school education, but suddenly he'd developed an all-powerful desire to be a medical doctor. The obstacles to his goal seemed, for a time, nearly insurmountable. He had a family of several children, he was operating his own business, and his age was against him.

But George Stanley was determined to win or perish. He earned a high school diploma by taking and passing a series of examinations. Then he enrolled in college and began to study toward his bachelor's degree. When he received his Bachelor of Arts he was 52 years old. Medical schools, he found, were reluctant ,to admit a student of that age. But Stanley, finally, through undaunted determination, convinced the dean of the Indiana University Medical School that he should be accepted as a student.

Now as a medical student he attempted to operate his cold storage plant and pursue his studies simultaneously. It was too much. He failed one semester and was dropped from the medical school. Stanley, however, was determined to become a doctor. He sold his business, enrolled in a master's degree program and for one semester made top grades now that he was relieved of the burden of running a full-time business on the side. He used the money from the sale of his business to support his family while he studied. With his record of excellent grades, the second time around, he again talked the medical school dean into permitting him to re-enter medical school.

Four years later, at the age of 56, George Stanley obtained his medical degree and became an intern at Mercy Hospital in San Diego, California. Then, after a year's internship, now age 57, he was a full-fledged, qualified and practicing doctor. . . .

When I emphasize desire, I'm referring to the kind George Stanley had. It's the kind you must have if you expect to succeed, and succeed big.

You can achieve anything you believe, but your realistic thoughts must be accompanied with deep feeling and desire. A wish isn't a belief, it certainly isn't a desire.

Now, just for a moment, imagine what you'd like to be and what you'd like to have. Ask yourself: Am I willing to do what is required to obtain them? If you answer "yes," then you have aroused in yourself a deep desire for them. To reinforce yourself ask these questions: Can I become enthusiastic about them? Will I constantly dwell upon them in my mind?

Then picture yourself, in your mind, as having the thing or things you most desire. Keep that mental image and draw upon it constantly.

If you'll do this, the image you've created will become more and more the real you. After a time, you'll find yourself actually playing the role of the person you intend to be. When you reach this point you're well on your way to success.

Let me return again to the subject of negative versus positive thought. If you're after success it's your purpose to concentrate upon what you want, what you desire; not upon what you don't want. That is, don't entertain the possibility of failure.

When the late U.S. Army Major General Verne D. Mudge planned and successfully executed the World War II military maneuver that liberated the Santo Tomas civilian internment camp and the Mayacayan Palace in Manila, I later asked him what would have happened if his tactics had failed?

"It would have been disastrous for the civilian prisoners," he said, "but I never allow myself to think in that way."

The point, of course, is that you shouldn't consider the possibility of defeat; envision only victory.

And once you've made your decision, established your goal, it's vital that you compel your conscious mind to pay strict attention to it; that nothing be permitted to interfere with your achieving your objective. In other words, keep your eye constantly on the target.

As an appropriate climax to this chapter, I wish to introduce one of the most unusual persons I've ever known. He's Staff Sergeant Robert L. De Barge, Sr., U.S. Marine Corps, retired.

De Barge is a man who knows, better than most, what it is to have a deep, compelling desire, and who believes you should never quit until you've obtained your goal, no matter what the odds. Fifteen years ago he lay in a military hospital in Japan without the ability to speak, read or write, His entire left side was paralyzed; he was incapable of walking or moving his left arm. The cells in the right side of his brain had died.

De Barge then could have looked forward only to a lifetime of invalidism, and, but for his determination, that could have been his future.

Nevertheless, today at 46 he lives a useful and happy life with his wife, Janet, and their two sons, Robert, Jr., 21, and Glenn, 7. The story that lies between is one of a courageous heart and the unending determination of a man who achieved an almost medical miracle. It all began on a dark January night in Korea in 1953. De Barge was leading his patrol.

"The Red Chinese were throwing hand grenades all over the place," he recalls. "The man on the point was wounded by one. I went to help him. Then there was a blinding flash and that is all I remember."

Two days later he awoke in a hospital. The grenade had exploded almost where he stood. Its fragments ripped into his throat, left shoulder and right hip and knee. He suffered flash burns on his face. The grenade had destroyed one of De Barge's vocal chords. It had severed the main blood artery to the right side of his brain.

For the next two years, in his words, "I learned to speak like a baby. I was in a wheel chair for six months, then on crutches for a month and then I began to walk with a cane."

"One night I was lying in the hospital and I needed to go to the bathroom," De Barge recalls. "I couldn't even get the medical corpsman's attention. I said to myself, 'I'm going to learn to walk again no matter what.' "

And learn he did. It took De Barge two years of learning to speak again with only one vocal chord. While he was learning to speak, he also was training himself to walk. Janet De Barge told of her husband's efforts, "He just never would quit, he has a lot of patience. He would keep trying over and over again."

De Barge today drives his car, mows the lawn, trims the hedges around his home and climbs a ladder to paint the eaves.

He summed up his philosophy this way: "When I trained young Marines I taught them never to give up. It was what the Marines taught me—and I believe it."

Desire, determination, and the refusal to quit—an unwillingness to accept, or even consider, defeat—paid dividends for Sergeant De Barge. They can do the same for you.

By now you may be thinking: "Is success really worth the effort? Night work and weekends on the job? Continuous pressure, study, dedication, long years of hard work before I have anything to show for it?"

If those are your thoughts, you've missed the point. If you'd talk to successful men you'd put your finger on it quickly. They, you'd learn, enjoy the struggle, the effort, the hard work, and the achievement that goes into striving for and attaining success. They find the pursuit of their goals fun. The day dreamer, the loser, won't understand this; it'll be apparent only to the person with the winner's philosophy.

The material rewards from success are comforting, they bring prestige and money, but even more important to the achiever, the winner, is his own feeling of self-satisfaction; that sense of personal accomplishment.

So, now that we've about come to the end of this chapter, let's review the essential points to convert wishes into reality:

First, you have to know what you want before you develop a plan and begin to act to achieve it. You must have an overriding, all-powerful, desire.

Second, you must establish for yourself an immediate goal, one you can achieve within six months or one year. You discard wishes and daydreams; you establish as your goal an objective for which you have an urgent desire.

Third, you don't wait for things to happen. You begin now to make them happen by study, by making realistic plans, by making contact with persons who can guide and help you, and by making those decisions that'll keep you on your target.

Fourth, you start now; not tomorrow, not next week. If you put off your plans and the action required to achieve what you desire, you'll never reach your goal.

Fifth, regardless of what obstacles confront you, you'll never quit until you achieve your goal. When the going gets tough, when you face discouragement and disappointment, you'll know that's the time to increase your concentration on your objective and work even harder. Then you'll develop staying power because as James Joseph Ling said, "It's the staying power that makes the difference between the winners and losers."

MILLIONAIRE SECRET #3

How to Set Up a Master Plan for Automatic Success

If you believe as I do that desire is the first key to success, then let's look closely at a man who agrees with us and has used the key to amass a fortune. This Californian dares to think he has discovered the elusive secret of financial success and how anyone can duplicate it if he has the desire to do so.

And so, the youthful man who sat across the luncheon table at the $4 million Le Baron Hotel in San Diego's Mission Valley was expensively tailored, trim, obviously physically fit, and the nails on his fingers were carefully manicured.

"As a boy I wanted to be wealthy and successful and I don't believe I've ever lost sight of those goals," he said. "Every chance I had I'd talk to successful men and find out how and what they did to make their fortunes."

"But I refused to listen to unsuccessful people's advice," he added.

That, admittedly capsulized, has been the success formula of Kenneth Robert Riley, "Ken" to his friends who are legion, a 35-year-old who's living proof a young man can still amass a million dollars—or more—if he has the desire and will take the action to do so.

Riley conservatively estimates his personal wealth at $3 million. He amassed it in 10 years. Not bad for a fellow who began his career from zero.

On a recent day, Ken Riley disclosed the master plan for automatic success that has brought him riches and countless achievements. It's a plan, he believes, that can be adopted and used by anyone who'll train himself for success and and make the necessary sacrifices.

As Riley sat, relaxed and confident, in the restaurant of the Le Baron Hotel, one of the many enterprises he owns and operates, the passerby would have observed a young, 158-pound, 5-feet 9-inch man with hazel eyes and brown hair. The passerby would never have stopped and said to himself, "There's a young millionaire who through a burning desire, a plan and a goal built himself a personal fortune of $3 million and today controls properties worth many millions more."

But that's precisely what Ken Riley has done from a modest start as a shipping clerk in a paint manufacturing company.

"There have been four major elements in any success I've achieved," Riley said. He outlined them:

"1. A burning desire and driving ambition to be wealthy.

"2. A tolerant and understanding wife, Melinda, without whom I couldn't have succeeded so rapidly.

"3. A book, *Law of Success* by Napoleon Hill, and

"4. An inspirational record, *Strangest Secret* by Earl Nightingale distributed by Success Motivation Institute, Inc., Waco, Texas.

"The really most important thing in my life to date," Riley said, "has been my burning desire to be wealthy and successful. This has brought me closer to my goal."

Riley has achieved his success on a foundation of a high school education plus two years at Pasadena City College where he majored in business education and finance. Beyond that he's self-taught.

So, then how does a man like Ken Riley, who has just completed a multi-million dollar hotel-restaurant complex, achieve such success?

"One must have a burning desire to succeed," he said, "In order to keep the 'burning desire' alive, a person must constantly be aware of it.

"Sit down and write out what you want in life," he advised. "Don't generalize, be specific. Don't say you'd like to make a lot of money. Put down what you want, and when you want it.

"Most people reflect money as business success, however, this doesn't have to be. Your 'burning desire' might be one like Albert Einstein's, but whatever it is, you must write it down and commit it to memory, imagine it, say it, practice it every single day.

"Set your goal high," Riley said, "at least five times more than you first thought. If you want to be worth $200,000 in 10 years, put down $1 million in 10 years. Believe it—once you have this 'burning desire' it's just as easy to make $1 million in 10 years as $200,000."

"How, specifically, should a person lay out his goal?" Riley was asked.

"Get a pen and a piece of paper and write it out," he replied. "For instance, do it this way:

I will be worth $1 million in 1982.

I will get this $1 million without sacrificing my health or happiness.

I will accomplish this by surrounding myself with the right people and the right things to do this job for me. *Example:* books, study courses, people; what I need, I'll get.

I'll be healthier by eating right, getting plenty of rest, no excessive drinking, getting plenty of exercise, and adapting my mind to take tension without causing physical damage to my body.

I'll be happier by controlling myself so that I'll be more tolerant and understanding of other people.

If need be, I'll work a 10-hour day, six days a week; I'll work to improve my personality, and I'll do whatever I can to have a closer relationship with my family.

And, finally, I'll keep my attitude and thinking calm and cheerful at all times.

I'm sure you'll agree, Ken Riley's plan is certainly a Master Plan for Automatic Success if there ever was one!

As he said, "When you set your big goal, you also must get your intermediate goals. In order to get to the top of the ladder, you must go 'step-by-step.' "

It's a formula, though, that's worked for Riley.

He began his step-by-step up the ladder in 1958 when he moved from California to Las Vegas, Nevada, and built himself a home. When it was finished he sold it and built another. This started him in the general contracting business. In 1959 he began construction of a 20-unit apartment house. He completed it and sold it in May 1960. For a time he was a member of a partnership, Luke and Riley Construction Company, Las Vegas. But in November 1961 he went into business on his own as K.R. Riley, General Contractor.

His first major project on his own was a $15 million Las Vegas complex of 1,200 apartments, three office buildings, 200,000 square feet of warehousing and a motel, the Villa Roma Motel, on Convention Center Drive about 800 feet from the Stardust Hotel, which he sold in 1967.

"This was started with no capital and no co-signers," Riley said.

After several years of successfully building and operating apartment houses, office buildings, warehouses and motels, Riley was set for his next step up the ladder. After much study and analysis, he decided the hotel business would be the most lucrative and challenging for him, "as well as the most difficult."

He began a self-study program that would equip him as an expert in all phases of the hotel business—financing, construction, furnishing, operating, and promotion.

"There are very few hotel companies which have all this experience plus a finished product," Riley said. "Because I do I can complete projects for less than my competitors can. By passing these savings on to hotel guests in the form of more reasonable rates I've been able to generate a higher volume of business."

It's such a philosophy that has caused Riley to be identified as a "positive thinker."

Riley said that on his way to success he learned "that you must have no negative thoughts, whatsoever. Negative thoughts cause negative results. Positive thoughts cause positive results. If you have a negative thought you should immediately replace it with a positive one."

He said he believes a major key to great success is a person's ability to "imagine himself successful. All great men have imagined themselves successful long before they became successful."

It doesn't take any extraordinary ability to succeed, Riley said, but a man must "do more than you get paid for and soon you'll be paid for more than you do."

He believes you can "do it if you believe you can," but he cautions that "you cannot succeed if you give up on any one of your intermediate goals."

Riley insists a person doesn't have to be a genius to make a fortune, but that he does have to sacrifice many things to achieve success.

"You must, for instance, spend long hours at work, read success books instead of watching television, and spend weekends at work and study instead of playing golf, swimming, or boating. You don't have to stop doing these things, but you must cut down on them. In later years, after you've achieved success, you can do anything in life you want without sacrificing."

Riley believes each person can, if he desires, gain control of his mind. "Then it acts as a machine to carry out your work."

Religion, in Riley's judgement, has played an important part in his achievements and he said that religion was "important to personal family life with children."

Ken Riley also believes in yoga and each morning and evening practices the method of transcendental meditations as taught by Maharishi Mahesh Yogi, the Indian mystic who teaches that mental poise, through meditation, is a state of equilibrium in which the mind, having absolute control, becomes a dynamic center of direct perception.

Maharishi himself has described his method this way:

> My aim is to bring the mind to a state in which it is no longer distracted by external matters. Once this is achieved, you've arrived at the true Self. The nature of the state is pure consciousness, total awareness, absolute being. You cease to become an individual but are simply aware of yourself as part of everything that exists.

Ken Riley's philosophy, however, isn't entirely based on Yoga Teachings. He's also a dedicated Christian.

"Prayer is most important to man's goal and success," he said. Riley believes his prayers are almost always answered and this gives him confidence in his God.

"I firmly believe these words," he said. "Ask and you shall receive, seek and you will find, and knock and it will be opened unto you."

Riley is what his employees and business associates term an "action man," that is, he's a fast mover and sometimes gets impatient when things don't move as rapidly as he'd like them to. As one of his associates said, "Ken hasn't any use for the negative thinker, the complainer, or the person without enthusiasm. He isn't easily satisfied and at times expects subordinates to do a thing exactly as he would do it."

Riley admits to at least one, perhaps minor, failing in dealing with his employees. "I don't always praise an employee when he's doing a basically good job."

Another of his associates said, "Sometimes he speaks too frankly to an employee when a little more tact could be used."

What's Ken Riley's goal for the future?

"I plan to build and operate 10 new hotels within the next 10 years; one each year with 500-room average, with assets of $75 million," he said, "I believe I could build 20 hotels in 10 years, but I'd have to sacrifice some of my family life, happiness and health, and it wouldn't be worth it, for money isn't my total goal."

Riley's on schedule with his goal. Not long ago, he opened his second hotel-restaurant complex in Burlingame, California, a suburb of San Francisco. It, too, is called the Le Baron Hotel, the same name as the one in San Diego. Located on Bay Shore Highway, three minutes by auto from the San Francisco International Airport, the new hotel has 175,000 square feet, 340 units, on four acres, with two cocktail lounges (one a Skyroom), a restaurant and a coffeeshop. It's 10 stories high and was built at a cost of $4.5 million.

The empire Riley has built and is building was started, as he said, "without a dime." He initially acquired capital from investors for construction projects in return for a percentage of each project. This was pyramided to his present level of financial success.

As for the tested money-making techniques he's used in his business, he says they're basically two: (1) You must be price conscious, that is, you must start from the beginning and build the finished product for less than your competitors. This means a smaller loan, a smaller debt, and it means you need less occupancy to break even on your hotel; if you accomplish this and your competition is high you're in a better position to lower your rates and offer the same as your competitors for less; and (2) You must know what your'e doing. This falls in line with setting your goal and with a goal you'll learn what you're doing.

Today Ken Riley sits in his plush office in his San Diego Le Baron Hotel and looks forward to his next project. And if you ask him to define his success formula, briefly, he'll tell you it has five essential points:

1. A burning desire to succeed.

2. Constantly putting your goal in front of you each day.

3. Positive thinking only.

4. It's just as easy to succeed as it is to fail.

5. You must have intermediate goals.

It's a formula that has made Ken Riley a millionaire three times over, and it's one he insists will work for you. And it begins with a burning, all-powerful, deep-seated, desire to achieve a specific goal you've set for yourself.

MILLIONAIRE SECRET #4

How to Put Your Master Plan into Motion

Rich Leon is a determined young man who wants to play professional football. Few of those who know him doubt that he'll achieve his goal and become a star split end among the pros.

Because it's desire—and action— that sets Rich Leon apart from the hundreds, perhaps thousands, of other college football players with the same ambition. It was an all-powerful desire bolstered by his willingness to act which got him back playing football after doctors told him he was through, and that he might even walk with a limp the remainder of his life.

Leon, who in 1968 was a 6-feet 1-inch, 192-pound split end at the University of Hawaii, was in 1966 punting for the University of Southern California against the University of Miami when a hard-charging Hurricane lineman snapped his right leg.

"They said I'd never play football again and I would walk with a limp from then on," Leon recalled.

Osteomyelitis, a bone infection, set in and made his condition worse. Doctors put his leg in a cast for nine months and a steel plate was inserted into his knee.

"That disease usually stays with you, so I didn't know what I was going to do. I was pretty discouraged," Leon said.

A near miracle occured, the disease slowed, and with the help of antibiotics, his leg began to respond. He talked the doctors into removing the steel plate from his knee and he began working to get his leg back into shape.

Put another way, Leon still had a desire to play football and he transmitted that deep-seated desire into action.

"I admit that daily training wasn't my idea of perfect peace," he said, "but I had to accept it." He worked long and hard—he took action. "I just ran and ran and ran. Later I was told that if I sat out a year, I might be able to play again. So I redshirted at USC and went out for the drills. I began to see the Trojans weren't going to be passing a lot."

Why should they pass? With possibly the outstanding runner in football history, O.J. Simpson, the USC team built its plans around the 207-pound halfback from San Francisco. This forced Leon to make still another decision. Although he'd grown up in Los Angeles, Leon decided he'd have to go elsewhere to play—somewhere where they'd throw the ball. So, again, he acted.

"I wrote 20 letters and Coach Dave Holmes (of Hawaii) was the only one to write me back," Leon recalled. "I decided then to go to Hawaii and I think it was a wise decision."

The fans in Hawaii agree.

In 1968 he caught 48 passes in nine games for 620 yards and six touchdowns. He also punted an average 36.9 yards per kick, many of which were short squib kicks to put the opponents back near their goal line.

So before long, as many predict, you'll find Rich Leon's name on the roster of a professional football team. It'll be there because of his desire and his willingness to do what he needed to do to succeed.

The point I'm making here, using Rich Leon as an example, is that nothing stops a man with an all-powerful desire plus the added element of being willing to act—the second key to success: putting your Master Plan into motion.

Leon could have accepted his physical impairment. He could have taken the doctors word that he'd walk with a limp the remainder of his life. He didn't though, and he did something about it.

But let's stop, briefly, and emphasize that action without thought, without a plan, is futile. A man who acts without thinking is a fool. So, again we start with a strong desire, a mapped Master Plan to achieve it, and then we act to put our Master Plan into motion.

To illustrate the need for a plan before you act, let's use an example. Suppose, for instance, you're after a specific job you strongly desire. What, then, are the steps, how do you plan, to land it?

First, decide precisely what kind of job you want. If it doesn't exist, perhaps you can create it.

Second, analyze the job's requirements. List them under separate headings of education, training, experience, license necessary, and so on.

Third, analyze yourself. Do you have the qualifications for the job? If not, outline what you need to do to obtain them.

Fourth, choose the industry, business, or profession in which you want to work at the occupation you've chosen for yourself.

Fifth, analyze the field you've chosen and determine how you can most attractively present what you have to offer the industry, business, or profession. Concentrate on the qualities you believe will separate you from the competition.

Sixth, prepare a resume pointing up your strongest qualifications—education, experience, training, past achievements, characteristics, and so forth.

Seventh, see that your resume is placed in the hands of those who have the authority to employ you.

When you get to step three, for instance, you may discover you haven't the qualifications for the job you seek. If so, you stop and create a plan to achieve them. It may call for you to map a program of self-study, enrollment in college, or you may have to sit for a license examination. Whatever you have to do, you'll do it if you have a strong enough desire for the job.

I believe I've made my point, but to repeat it, you can't act until you've made a thorough, detailed, and constructive Master Plan.

Okay, you say, suppose I map plans to achieve what I desire and then act on them; how do I know I'm taking the correct action?

You'll know when there remains no question in your mind that you've done the best you're capable of to create your plans. Your plan may be far from perfect, but execute it with enthusiasm. There's a military axiom: "A poor plan well executed is much better than a good plan poorly executed." Battles have been won on this premise. It works in the life and death crisis of the battlefield, and so it'll work for you.

I have watched people make decisions and execute plans which, according to others' evaluation of them, were mistakes, but which were executed with such conviction and enthusiasm that they worked. They worked because of the tremendous effort and enthusiasm put into them. Conviction had the power of releasing such great effort.

Let's, for instance, look at the career of S. S. McClure, who revolutionized American journalism by introducing syndicated material to metropolitan newspapers. His plan was to sell literary material by the most popular writers of the day to the newspapers; to sell a short story for which he'd paid, say, $100, to 50 newspapers at $5 apiece, and so make a profit. His friends, fellow journalists and others told him that anyone who attempted such an enterprise was demented.

And although he had little money, only enough to print some stationary and pay a month's rent on an office, he signed up some of the nation's best known authors as contributors. Then he took to the road and personally sold newspaper editors on his new service.

Ultimately, McClure had the biggest and most profitable newspaper syndicate in the nation. Within six years after he'd launched his enterprise, he was publishing "McClure's Magazine," which from 1890 to 1915 was the most exciting, the liveliest, the best illustrated, the most attractive, the most interesting, and the most profitable national magazine of the period.

But at the start, McClure had only his own conviction to sustain him, but it was enough. He laid his plans and through action he successfully executed them.

The characteristics McClure displayed are as successful today as they were then.

The point I'm making is this: If you believe you can do something, you have a fighting chance of doing it. That's essential. You may fail, but that's the risk you must take. Otherwise, you remain among the ranks of the losers, frozen there with doubt and fear.

If you fail, then you should "get back on the horse;" that is, try again. It's important to remember that life, more often than not, affords you second chances. Opportunity rarely appears but once. It's also true that the man of action, who plans, makes his own opportunities more often than not.

Ultimately it's the doer who counts. For as President Theodore Roosevelt once said: "It is not the critic who counts, not the man who points out how the strong man stumbled or where the doer of deeds could have done better. The credit belongs to the man who is actually in the arena; whose face is marred by dust and sweat and blood; who strives valiantly, who errs and comes up short again and again; who knows the great enthusiasms, the great devotions, and spends himself in a worthy cause; who at the best knows in the end the triumph of high achievement; and who at the worst, if he fails, at least fails while daring greatly; so that his place shall never be with those cold and timid souls who know neither defeat nor victory."

So, you'll make mistakes; but most of them will not in themselves be terribly important in the long run. You should even allow yourself a certain amount of room for error, for impulse, for sheer spontaneity.

If you'll accept this premise, you'll find that doing something—taking action—about your problems can banish doubt. If you're willing to be wrong rather than simply doubtful, you'll venture more and enjoy the satisfaction of learning from your experience as well as ultimately achieving success.

I believe, firmly, that sound planning, based on an all-powerful desire, and backed up by action, plants the seeds of success.

But, you ask, how do I start; when do I start to act?

You start now. You can become a man of action this moment simply by putting aside this book, temporarily, picking up a piece of paper and a pen and writing out what your goal in life is and your plan of action to achieve it.

That act, in itself, would immediately place you in the ranks of the winners—the men who control their own destinies, who know what they want, and how they're going to go about getting it.

Your Master Plan, in most cases, will require change— change in your attitudes, job, perhaps location, associations, and so on. But don't fear change. Don't become a victim of job security. You can, for instance, easily rationalize your immobility, your lack of flexibility, in terms of "family responsibilities." If you do, you'll find yourself leaning more and more on job security—you'll lean on it because you're personally insecure.

You needn't fall into this trap; not when you realize that your true security is what's in your head. Not when you've mustered self-confidence, by reaching out for new and varied experience; by practicing self-improvement and taking specialized training courses; by developing and using creative thinking; and by putting in more thought-hours than the next fellow.

It's vital to remember that once you bolster your native ability with practical experience and useful knowledge, you become a valuable commodity on the labor market. You become your own security; that's the solid foundation on which you build big money fast.

Then, once you've acquired this lining of inner confidence, the prospect of change won't frighten you. You'll quickly learn that change breeds challenges. And it's the challenges that spur you on up your ladder of success.

Perhaps you believe that because of where you live you have no challenges, no opportunities, to help you succeed. Where you live actually has nothing to do, initially, with your making your plan for success and then acting. It's your desire, your resolution, that counts. Abraham Lincoln pointed this out to a young man, Isham Reavis, who'd written Lincoln for advice. This is Lincoln's reply:

> My dear Sir:
>
> I have just reached home and found your letter. If you are resolutely determined to make a lawyer of yourself, the thing is more than half done already. It is but a small matter whether you read with anybody or not. I did not read with anyone. Get the books and read and study them till you understand them in their principal features, and that is the main thing. It is of no consequence to be in a large town while you are reading. I read at New Salem, which never had three hundred people living in it. The books, and your capacity for understanding them, are just the same in all places.
>
> Always bear in mind that your own resolution to succeed is more important than any other one thing.
>
> A. Lincoln

Lincoln's key to success was simply this: "Your own resolution to succeed is more important than any other one thing." Your resolution, your conviction, then, is what counts; backed up by well-thought-out plans implemented by direct action. But on this matter of resolution, or conviction, let me say that ultimately a man sets the measure of his own success by the level at which he chooses to establish his convictions.

If, for example, you have a conviction that whatever you do "things will go wrong," then you've set up a conviction that works against you instead of for you. So think good thoughts—positive ones—because they'll attract good things.

If you order your life, your future, in terms on many special and inflexible convictions about temporary matters you make yourself the victim of circumstances. I always ask myself this question when I'm tempted to establish a conviction on a temporary matter: Will it be important to me a year from now? If it won't, I don't worry about it. I do this because I know that each little prior conviction that isn't open to review is a hostage that I give to the future; it determines whether the events of tomorrow will bring me happiness or misery.

For instance, if you haven't the education needed to obtain the job you seek, but nevertheless you've convinced yourself you can't succeed without more knowledge, then you've let a temporary matter make you a victim of circumstances. If you have the strong desire you can overcome the temporary problem by working out and executing a plan to better educate yourself.

So, if you truly want to succeed, encompass your convictions in a broad perspective; that is, cast them in terms of principles rather than rules. If you do, you'll find you have a much better chance of discovering those alternatives which will lead eventually to your success. Avoid castiron rules, instead apply theories.

Let's look at it this way: You're a prisoner of your convictions, a hostage of two contradictory beliefs. You believe, on the one hand, that there must be greater success, more worthwhile experiences than you currently know, which might enable you to devise for yourself a more productive, and fruitful life; yet you feel obliged, on the other hand, to dismiss such possible success and experiences as unnecessary and even as unreal. Therefore, you've made a castiron rule for yourself, which is, "those things are for others, I don't need them." That's defeatism based upon an invalid rule. Instead, you should adopt a theory such as: "Everyone is entitled to whatever success and achievement he can realize through his own desire, capacity, and action." I believe this makes the point.

Theories, then, are the thinking of men who seek success, mobility, and flexibility amid swirling events. The theories comprise prior assumptions about certain facets of these events, or circumstances. So, to that extent, the events may, from these prior assumptions, be construed, predicted, and their relative courses charted. Thus you can exercise control and achieve what you're after.

If you adopt a broad theory such as, "I can achieve anything for which I have an all-powerful desire," then this assumption, a prior one made by you, will enable you to predict the outcome of the events in which you become involved.

To achieve this flexibility of thinking it takes action—mental action to assure yourself that you don't fill your brain with narrow-minded thoughts, prejudices, out-dated ideas and concepts. Instead, you should ask yourself these questions about your convictions: Is there any rational reason for my belief? Would I come to the same conclusion about some other person in a similar situation? Why should I continue to act and feel as if this were true if there is no valid reason to believe it?

With this technique, you avoid jumping to conclusions based on half-truths, incomplete thoughts, and the making of judgements from prejudice. You avoid misevaluations.

The late Alfred Korzybski, author of *Science and Sanity* and an internationally known semanticist used a procedure in his seminars to demonstrate how easily you can make a misevaluation. He would pick a young woman student and prearrange with her a demonstration about which the class knew nothing. At a point in his lecture Korzybski would call the young woman to the platform and hand her a box of matches. She would take them carelessly and drop them to the floor. That was the only "crime" she committed. Korzybski would begin to call her names with a display of anger, waving his fists in front of her face, and finally with the big gesture, he'd slap her face gently.

"Seeing this 'slap', as a rule 90 percent of the students would recoil and shiver; 10 percent would show no overt reaction," Korzybski said. "The latter had seen what they had seen, but they delayed their evaluations. Then I explained to the students that their recoil and shiver was an organismal evaluation very harmful in principle, because they identified the seen facts with their judgements, creeds, dogmas, etc. Thus their reactions were entirely unjustified, as what they had seen turned out to be merely a scientific demonstration of the mechanism of identification, which identification I expected."

The point then is that you must have all the information you can obtain before you make a judgement, come to an evaluation; otherwise you can make serious errors in your thought processes.

You read, for instance there is much discrimination today on the basis of age for job-hunters; particularly for persons over 40. But does this mean a man over 40 can't get a job? Of course not. You can verify this daily by reading in your daily newspaper about men of 50,60, even 70 being appointed to new positions. Therefore, if you say, "I'm over 40 and am no longer employable at my trade or profession," you have a belief with no valid reason behind it.

Since you intend to act on your beliefs, your thinking processes, it's important to use the power of rational thinking. And remember, ideas are changed by other ideas.

Is it possible, you ask, to change my life, my total outlook, through the act of rational thinking? Bertram Russell, the English philosopher and scientist, said he did it in five minutes one day in 1901. He described the process in Volume I of *The Autobiography of Bertram Russell:*

> Within five minutes I went through some such reflections as the following: the loneliness of the human soul is unendurable; nothing can penetrate it except the highest

intensity of the sort of love that religious teachers have preached; whatever does not spring from this motive is harmful, or at least useless; it follows that war is wrong, that a public (private) school education is abominable, that the use of force is to be deprecated, and that in human relations one should penetrate to the core the loneliness in each person and speak to that.

Lord Russell said that at the end of that five minutes of thought he'd become a completely different person.

> I felt that I knew the inmost thought of everyone that I met on the street, and though this was, no doubt, a delusion, I did in actual fact find myself in far closer touch than previously with all my friends, and many of my acquaintances ... I found myself filled with semi-mystical feelings about beauty, with an intense interest in children, and with a desire almost as profound as that of the Buddha to find some philosophy which should make human life endurable. A strange excitement possessed me, containing intense pain but also some element of triumph through the fact that I could dominate pain, and make it, as I thought, a gateway to wisdom. . . .

The point, then, that I've made in this chapter is simply this: The ability to come up with new and better solutions to problems depends on thinking them through clearly, and then acting—executing the solution, the decision, at which you've arrived.

Try it, it works.

Remember, however, you shouldn't waste your time in idle, worthless, thought. Eliminate daydreams; concentrate instead on the immediate, practical problem that confronts you. Steer yourself to a decision, then act.

That's precisely what Rich Leon did after doctors told him he'd never again play football and probably would walk the rest of his life with a limp because of his injury.

Leon refused to accept that. Instead, through desire and action he solved his problem: He had the unending urge to win, and he did.

So can you.

MILLIONAIRE SECRET #5

How to Use the Magic Formula
that Makes the "Breaks"
Come Your Way

Honolulu's William Koon Hee
Mau is a man of action who's always been willing to take a
calculated risk. This characteristic has been the solid rock
foundation on which Bill Mau parlayed a hamburger stand and a
Chinese restaurant into a financial empire that has made him a
multi-millionaire and one of Hawaii's greatest success stories.

"You can make a million dollars, too," Mau told me.

What he meant was that you too can make it if you're willing
to use similar techniques and make the same sacrifices he did.

In 25 years Mau rose from a U.S. Civil Service clerk-typist to
a financier with a net worth of more than $13 million. His
annual salary is reputed to be $500,000.

As some Honolulu people put it, Mau has "caused more
commotion in town than anything since the Japanese attack on
Pearl Harbor."

His Hawaiian friends call him a "keiki o ka aina" . . . son of
the land. His business associates know him as an astute financier
who seldom misses the "big" opportunities. And his intimates
remember that Bill Mau rose from abject poverty to become
one of the most affluent citizens of the Hawaiian Islands.

What, then, enabled Bill Mau to climb so rapidly to success? It wasn't black magic, and it wasn't blind luck. The answer lies in three areas.

First, Bill Mau has always kept a tight grip on his own destiny. He wanted to make a success of his life and he knew it was in his power to do so. He set his goal, made his plans, and took the required action to achieve it.

Second, he disciplined himself. He spends more time at his work even today than most other men do. Mau has never stopped searching for new ideas. He has done everything possible to encourage "breaks" to come his way, and he's kept his thinking flexible so he could take advantage of the "breaks".

Third, Bill Mau learned early in his career that it was vital to his success to be able to sell his ideas to other people.

Mau said he earned his fortune acting on the principle of the Golden Rule, doing unto others as he would have them do unto him. He believes this with fierce intensity, just as he believes God created man to live among his neighbors, regardless of race, creed or religion.

Jack H. McDonald, president of the billion-dollar San Diego Imperial Corporation, and a business associate of Mau's, said, "Bill Mau is more than an idealist or dreamer, he's a doer—he acts. He's the kind of man who has risen above the pettiness of today's business world to accomplish what seemingly has been the impossible."

Mau himself never thought of his ambitions as being impossible. But to many another boy born into Bill Mau's circumstances they probably would have been. He credits his success to shrewd investments, good timing and what he likes to call "just plain luck".

It has taken more than luck, though, to catapult this Chinese-American banker into the forefront of Hawaii's booming economy. Perseverence—staying power, Mau believes, has been one of the big-money secrets that has helped him in his inexorable climb to millionaire status.

The will to persevere, he said, enabled him to survive the near-starvation existence to which he was born in the old Duck Pond area not far from the glamorous Waikiki Beach. There, with his seven brothers and sisters, Mau lived in squalor.

"There were many times when we existed on only one meal a day, and it was scanty," Mau said.

Today at the age of 54 Mau owns the newly-completed $7.5 million, 19-story Ambassador Hotel, the 20-story Waikiki Business Plaza Building, he is chairman of the board and principal owner of Honolulu's American Security Bank, and he has wide real estate and other business interests in Hawaii and Hong Kong, the Empress Hotel there, for instance.

From the start Bill Mau made it easy for opportunity to find him. He learned as a high school boy that it was vital that he meet and get to know those who could help him.

Mau believes his first "break" came during his high school days in the early 1930s when he became a golf caddy.

"The advice I received when I caddied helped shape my future," he said. "The men I caddied for encouraged me to think seriously about getting steady employment after I graduated from high school. The lead for my first job, that of an elevator operator, was supplied by one of my golf customers."

He took the elevator operator's job at $65 a month in the old Hawaiian Trust Building. And as an elevator operator, Mau came into contact with even more of Hawaii's businessmen. One of them was to influence Mau's destiny. Mau recalled the incident:

"When it came time for my annual raise, he bluntly told me I was too good for the job. He said I should go out and find something better for myself. I took his advice."

Mau had in the days he worked as a caddy set for himself the goal of being successful and wealthy. He never once lost sight of his goal.

So, the next stop of Mau's relentless pursuit of success was a Honolulu advertising agency. He spent three years in it learning creative techniques that later served him as a real estate developer and businessman. Besides that, he earned $10 more a month than he had as an elevator operator.

By 1941 Mau could see no further opportunity for himself in the advertising agency. He quit and took a job as a clerk-typist in the Unemployment Division of the U.S. Department of Labor office in Honolulu. He rose progressively through the ranks to become a wages-and-hours inspector, and incidentally, to learn more about business life in Honlulu.

Mau kept his eyes on his goal—the achievement of wealth, position and influence.

With his savings, plus borrowed money, Bill Mau in 1941 acquired control of a hamburger stand on Waikiki's Kuhio Beach opposite the Surfrider Hotel. His wife, Jean, helped operate it. Bill Mau worked at his Civil Service job during the day and manned the hamburger stand at night.

"When I think back to those days," he said, "about all I can remember is the pungent odor of fried onions and the endless stream of catsup on thousands of hamburgers. Sometimes I think Jean and I helped feed the entire U.S. Pacific Fleet."

The 14-to-18 hour days Bill Mau worked, however, kept ringing the cash register until by 1949 his original $10,000 investment had increased to $100,000. In 1946 he left his Civil Service job to devote full-time to the hamburger stand and to work on the fringes of real estate. He bought and sold property in a series of quick cash deals.

If there is one day in Mau's life on which his destiny was decided it was when he gained at public auction the control of five million square feet of land in the Halawa area overlooking Pearl Harbor.

'I sold that land for 37½ cents a square foot," Mau recalled, "and prayed nightly that I would realize a 10-cent profit on each foot. By the end of six months, Halawa subdivision was sold out and I was richer by $500,000."

Mau modestly says he was "lucky" in obtaining the Halawa land and selling it so quickly. The facts are, however, that Mau studied the real estate market, he constantly searched for good buys, and he improved his knowledge of how to merchandise land. When the opportunity came, he was prepared for it.

And now as Mau's real estate ventures began to pay, he sought diversifications for his investments. With $200,000 of the $500,000 he'd earned in his first major real estate project, he bought Tropical Enterprises, Limited. With the purchase price was included the world-famous Lau Yee Chai Restaurant, considered a "must" eating place by tourists to Honolulu. Today the original Lau Yee Chai Restaurant is no more. Mau razed it to make way for his Ambassador Hotel.

Bill Mau continued to concentrate on his goal and he looked for other investment opportunities. A major one came in 1958 when he bought 12½ percent of the American Security Bank stock for $200,000. The bank was almost exclusively Chinese; Mau changed that immediately. He added members of other ethnic groups to the board of directors, hired Caucasian employees and swiftly moved the bank into position to serve the entire Honolulu business community.

Mau, on his way to financial success, has adhered to one basic philosophy—it's up to the individual to help himself. Beyond that, he believes God plays an active role in the life of every man. This philosophy comes from a man who admits he isn't deeply religious, nevertheless he's temperate and neither smokes nor drinks.

Moderate in his personal life, Mau is anything but staid in his business life. His combined projects represent 10 percent of the overall building outlays in Honolulu.

Does Mau believe a young man of today can start from scratch and achieve the same wealth he has in 25 years?

"Yes," Mau said, "he can, but he must have gumption, fortitude and a willingness to work."

He said it all depends on attitude and incentive to learn. Mau insists that if a man applies himself, and is willing to work long hours (in his case 14 to 16 hours daily, which he still does) he can get ahead, and accomplish anything he believes he can.

"Basically," Mau said, "I'm a man with ideas. I believe in letting others work out the rudiments of a problem. When I step in, I want to look at a project that is proving itself."

That's the way it is today for Bill Mau, but for many years he was a man with ideas who had to personally execute them, there wasn't a staff of experts around to help as there is now.

Today Bill Mau's "look" at his various projects starts daily at 6 a.m. After breakfast with four of his five children who live at home, he delivers them to school, then drives himself to his office for the beginning of another day of meetings. This series of conferences generally lasts well into the evening when Mau returns home to discuss the day's activities with his wife, Jean.

If Mau is an ideaman, and he is, then specifically how has he applied ideas to help him achieve even greater success?

Let's look at how he approached his project of making his American Security Bank more successful. This is his "magic formula" in his own words:

> Too often, bankers in the past have been content to wait for customers to approach them, and even then make them sweat and squirm when doing business with them. Today, that is about as suitable as the horse and buggy. We have to go out and try to catch the prospective customer, convince him that we can be of help to him, and give him cheerful, unfailing service at every step—or we will surely lose him to a more alert banker down the street.

In other words, Mau believes that once you have a new idea or service you must go out and sell it to others if you want success.

Shortly after Mau took over the bank, he decided to move its headquarters to Waikiki from "old" downtown Honolulu. Mau explained the idea behind the move:

> There seemed to be no reason against the move except time-honored custom. In the old days, when most money transactions were done in person, and in cash, there may have

been a decisive advantage in being close to the biggest
concentration of large commercial firms—in this case, Hawaii's
Big Five. But today, all this hardly applies any longer—and
there are on the other hand some advantages in being located
in Waikiki.

In assessing his own success, as that of any business, Mau
subscribes to the view that cash flow is more important than net
worth. This is one of the chief motivations behind many of his
moves, such as the development of income-producing proper-
ties.

Put another way, it's not how much money you're actually
worth that counts, but rather how much money you have to use
to increase your investments.

"The normal pattern in capital appreciation is that invested
money doubles in value after about eight years," Mau said, "but
if you really work at it, you can do it in half the time."

He believes that to succeed a man must constantly look for
new opportunities and then capitalize on them when they arise.
Mau thinks the State of Hawaii offers one of these opportunities.

"In 10 years," he said, "tourism will employ one-sixth of the
labor force in our state (Hawaii), and 1½ million tourists will
invade Waikiki annually, leaving behind probably a billion
dollars. That's what the economists say, and today it sounds
just as incredible as if someone had predicted, a few years ago,
that the son of a penniless immigrant would one day run $100
million worth of enterprises from the 20th floor of the Waikiki
Business Plaza. But since I've seen the one happen, I can easily
believe the other."

Mau believes part of his success that has enabled him to
control $100 million worth of enterprises has depended on his
program of self-study. With only a high school education behind
him, Mau has earned a fortune. He built his vast knowledge of
finance by reading and studying books on business, finance, and
banking, by talking with successful real estate men, and he said

he absorbed as much as he could "in my daily contacts with people involved in these fields."

More than the pursuit of money, however, occupies Mau's interests. He's a strong community leader. Some of his business associates say he's now interested in putting his talents and energy to work in helping the United States in its relations with foreign countries—particularly Asia. On this Mau said:

> As an American I would be willing to contribute in any way in which my knowledge can be of help. Because Hawaii is so strategically located I think men of Hawaii could be of value in Asian areas, but it would be a mistake to send a Chinese to Japan or vice versa. I do, however, believe I could be a good representative and better present the East-West philosophy than some New York 'Haole', (outsider), who, in my opinion, would be a total flop.

Domiciled today in his six-bedroom, $125,000 home in the Wilhelmina Rise section of Honolulu overlooking Diamond Head are his wife and daughters, Cynthia, Lynette, and Letitia, as well as Leighton, one of his two sons.

His home has one decided advantage—it affords him an unrestricted view of his "dream", the Waikiki Business Plaza, a product of his own imagination, the achievement of one of his goals.

And, while Mau's friends consider him the brightest financial star in the Hawaiian heavens, the 5-feet 9-inch, 168-pound Chinese—American knows that two essential characteristics possessed by him give him what he has—the motivation to act and the willingness to take a calculated risk.

It's a success story that Mau himself insists you can repeat if you have the all-powerful desire to do so and if you're willing, as he was, to act to reach your goal.

MILLIONAIRE SECRET #6

How to Develop a Winning Image that Makes Others Do What You Want

It's easy to rationalize your failure. You can say to yourself, "I can't take the risk to do that, it'll sacrifice my security." You can protest that my thesis in this book is unrealistic—that it couldn't possibly work for you.

But I assure you that realism is what this book is all about. I know the effort it takes, the risks involved, to make a hard decision in the face of what seem like overwhelming odds. But I know it can be done and that it is done by those who succeed. The winners override fear and doubt.

So far I've discussed with you the vital importance of an all-powerful desire (goal) backed up by thought-out action. But in adopting these two keys to success—desire and action—it's essential that you rid yourself of fear. That is, you must drive negative thoughts from your mind. You mustn't permit false beliefs, unrealistic rationalization, to halt your drive toward success. You must create a "winning image" within your mind.

Let's look at how false beliefs can stymie you and block your path to achievement:

Do you at the moment, for instance, believe your life is empty because you're an inferior person who's never done anything worthwhile and never will? If you do, then you're the victim of a negative, a false belief.

Simply turn that false belief into a realistic, positive one. Say to yourself, "I'm the equal of any man, I have within me the capacity to achieve whatever I desire, and I intend to do just that."

What I'm suggesting is that you take, one by one, each belief you hold that helps you rationalize your present circumstances and turn it around. When you do, you'll quickly, almost instantly, begin to develop an improved self-image, a winning image, of yourself.

Let's suppose you currently hold these false beliefs: I must suffer to atone for the mistakes I've made. My life has no meaning because I've lost my wife. In this nuclear age there's no point in my attempting to achieve anything, it could all be blown to oblivion in a second.

Now switch them around into positive thoughts, this way: I've learned from the mistakes I've made. I won't repeat them, but having made them gives me a broader experience that'll eventually help me achieve my goal. My wife is gone and no matter how I'd like to relive the past I know I can't; therefore, I must, as a debt to myself, look to the future. Since I personally have no control over the nuclear bomb, I can't let it influence my thoughts or my future.

So, declare war, right now, on your negative thoughts. As quickly as you do, you'll find that your fear of the future, of insecurity, of defeat, will rapidly dissipate.

Let's consider how one man did it.

Carl E. Herring, of Dallas, Texas, in 1957 set for himself the goal of becoming a United States Marine. It took an 11-year battle of determination, against almost insurmountable obstacles to achieve it. Today he's 28, married and the father of two children, but he's a Marine. He refused to permit fear and doubt to veer him from his course.

The obstacles to his goal, however, developed almost from the moment he arrived in San Diego in 1957 to begin training at the Marine Corps Recruit Depot. He broke his knee on the obstacle course. The knee refused to heal properly. After a series of treatments, Herring was medically discharged.

What would have been the end of the road for many was for Herring the beginning of his 11-year fight to wear the Marine uniform. He flooded the Marine Corps with letters requesting a waiver so he could re-enter the service. The Marine Corps finally said "yes," but on the condition that Herring pass physical requirements.

Herring had his knee operated on at his own expense and in June, 1968, he re-enlisted. Misfortune followed him. For on July 7, 1968, Herring broke his arm and was transferred from his training platoon into a medical rehabilitation platoon. That accident, too, he overcame.

Misfortune hadn't yet finished with Herring. After his broken arm healed, he went home on leave. He returned to his training platoon on July 27 and on the following day he was taken to the hospital suffering with meningitis. The hospital discharged him on October 16, 1968, and he was, now for the fourth time, given a chance to complete the training he'd begun 11 years earlier.

Finally, on Monday, December 9, 1968, Herring successfully completed his training and became a full-fledged U.S. Marine.

Repeatedly along the road to his goal, Herring could have, with some justification, adopted false beliefs. Certainly he could have decided he was "accident prone" and because of that would never have become a Marine. Later, after he married and became the father of two children, he could have pleaded "family responsibilities" to relinquish his goal. He could have become a victim of frustration.

But Herring fell victim to none of these false beliefs. And neither must you.

What, you ask, determines positive rather than negative beliefs?

In one word, I answer, attitude. Your attitude colors your whole approach to living. It works for or against you. It builds your career, or holds it down. But the important thing is that it's in your control.

We know that as members of the human species, we're by far the best thinkers in the animal kingdom—that's what sets us apart and above the lower forms of life. Our brain structure is extraordinary, it can't be duplicated by the most sophisticated of computers. In addition, we have the power of speech which enables us to think with others, enormously enlarging the scope of our problem-solving ability.

What can you do with these abilities?

First, you can take apart the elements of a problem confronting you and then consider each element separately and in relation to each other.

Second, you can consider alternative solutions.

Third, you can vary relevant influences hypothetically and in reality.

Fourth, you can weigh the desirability of one solution over another through a variety of methods; imagination, guessing, prediction, remembering, and you can add, subtract, divide, multiply so as to form new rules, new concepts.

So, I ask you: With your ability to do this why should you permit yourself false beliefs or the destructive elements of fear and doubt?

Doubt, I believe, comes from fear. But first, let's define doubt. It means to waver in opinion or judgment. It means to feel uncertain; to question things. It develops from defects in knowledge or evidence, it's an unrealistic viewpoint. Doubt also means the lack of confidence, the suspicion, the dread, the stopping of action which would bring you satisfaction and the fulfillment of your goal.

Since I said I believe doubt comes from fear, let's briefly, analyze fear. It's caused basically by those things we know less about. We tend to fear the unexpectedly strange. If, then, you have a good self-image, self-confidence, you'll seek constantly to study and learn about that which is strange to you. When you do this, you'll overcome fear and once you've overcome fear, you'll overcome doubt.

Let's, for a moment, look at the classic doubter in all literature: Hamlet. One moment he wants to die, but then he asks the classic questions of doubt: "To be or not to be: that is the question." Then, momentarily, he again chooses death. But hesitancy returns. Ultimately it was Hamlet's indecisiveness that brought about his destruction.

Now, briefly, let's look at the contrast—the man of action who achieves his goal of success. He's likely to see things in what may appear to his associates to be an over-simplified manner. He consolidates all the possible perspectives in terms of one two-sided issue. Then he makes his choice between the only two alternatives he allows himself to perceive. That is, he says to himself, "This is the crux of the various issues I've been considering, and for the time being, I'll deal with my problem as if it were this and only this." In other words, he selects what he believes to be the critical issue and disregards the relevancy of all the other issues involved. He creates a "winning image" in his mind.

If you'll use this method you'll find it makes your problems manageable and it gives you control of them. But, one caution: Be sure before you decide upon your two alternatives that you've reached them on the basis of accurate information and realistic judgment.

As I said earlier in this chapter, the elimination of fear and doubt and the creation of positive thoughts is deep-seated in your attitude. Every step forward in business, science, industry, the professions, the arts, has been the result of some person's positive attitude.

A brief look at a historical figure makes my point. The man in question spoke one sentence that'll live in the minds and hearts of Americans as long as the United States endures, and even beyond. Yet Patrick Henry, who believed in the power of any man to raise himself, began his adulthood with little education and no money. He set up a store and failed. At 18 he married a girl who brought him a small plantation, but he failed as a farmer. He went back to store-keeping, but failed for the third time.

By the time he was 23 he had four children, burdensome debts, no special training; however, he did have an endless number of friends, a superior memory, a logical mind and quick wits.

What could he do to make himself a success? he asked. The answer: become a lawyer; but how, without time or money, could he study law?

He borrowed a set of law books and had consumed their contents within six weeks. Then he traveled to Williamsburg, the colonial capital of Virginia, and presented himself for examination. He passed and was admitted to the Virginia Bar.

Young Patrick Henry returned to his hometown. With the help of his legion of friends he quickly built a large law practice. Within four years he was elected to the House of Burgesses and began a career that would make his name live forever. And it was on a March day in 1775 that Patrick Henry rose in the lower house of the Virginia colonial legislature and made his speech that contained the immortal sentence: "Forbid it, Almighty God! I know not what course others may take, but as for me, give me liberty or give me death!"

His words on that day sparked a fire in the breasts of men who, above all else, choose freedom.

Patrick Henry's life, and his achievements, proved, without qualification, that a man with an all-powerful desire, a man with a "winning image", who would act, and who never took counsel of doubt or fear, could with staying power, even though self-educated and a three-time failure, surmount all obstacles and become immortal.

These principles worked for Patrick Henry, and they'll work for you as they also worked for multi-millionaire Fred Lazarus, Jr., of New York, the 5-feet 2-inch man who built Federated Department Stores, Inc. into the world's largest department store group.

At the age of seven Fred Lazarus earned money to help the family finances of a friend by rising at 5 a.m. to grind and sell horse-radish and other condiments.

"You could see what a penny meant in that business," he later recalled. "If you sold 15 cents worth, that was a lot."

Later he began to work at F.R. Lazarus & Sons, the store founded by his grandfather in 1851. He started selling collars, relying on a stool to help him see over the counter, and earning 25 cents for a full day's work.

It was from such experiences that Lazarus said he learned the lessons of cost cutting that played a major role in Federated's growth. But it was his staying power, his constant study, and his all-powerful desire to succeed that propelled Lazarus into one of the giants of retailing.

He learned, for instance, that "you've got to have the right thing to sell, in the right surroundings, and at the right price. But you've got to be able to handle it so that you'll have enough left to expand your business."

Lazarus today, as in the past, keeps a watchful eye on the complaint department, recalling the days when his father ran the store with a system of mirrors that enabled him to see when a salesperson wasn't being properly attentive.

"The customer is my closest friend," Lazarus said, "People want to be treated pleasantly and knowledgeable and they have a right to it." He reserves a special fury for the salesperson who slights a customer. "Why, the first person I discharged was a glove buyer who refused to fit a Negro customer," he recalled. "Everyone's entitled to be treated properly—we have the same needs and the same money."

Lazarus calls flexibility and openness to the customer's needs the key qualities of a successful retailer.

"I've made some mistakes—some big ones," he said, recalling the time he bought all the separate collars a manufacturer had on hand. "It seemed like a great bargain, but we couldn't give them away. If you're going to make mistakes, just make sure you wind up on the right side of the ledger."

Lazarus is a successful man who's never harbored doubts or fears. His positive attitude has made him a multi-millionaire, and his "winning image" has made others do what he wants. You can do the same, if you can overcome your doubts and fears.

How then, you ask, can you conquer these doubts and fears so that you'll become a practicing exponent of positive thoughts and a success-oriented attitude?

You'll agree, I believe, that first you'll want to eliminate anxiety. If you can achieve this then you'll come close to conquering your fears and doubts. The best way to eliminate anxiety is to emphasize the mobility of your will (mind) and you can best do this by redefining truth and reality for yourself. I suggest you do this along the lines first proposed by the 17th Century subjectivist philosopher George Berkeley. He insisted that matter cannot be conceived independent of the mind. In other words, matter exists only to the extent that man perceives it. Since there is no external world, he argued, the phenomena of sense can be explained only by supposing a God which continually and coherently evokes perception in the mind of man.

Put another way, Berkeley theorized that you really don't have any evidence for the view that there is a world outside; all you have are the ideas of things. For instance, you have only an idea that this book exists because only through your own mind can you appreciate its existence. For you, the existence of the book is something you must subjectively establish for yourself, so that truth itself is your truth, my truth, or the truth of others. You are, then, what you believe yourself to be.

You may decide Berkeley's theory is amusing, yet the fact is that it's a philosophical system which has never been entirely refuted. And it is because of his system that Berkeley is considered one of the three or four most important English philosophers and as among the most important of all modern philosophers.

Berkeley's approach has special importance for you because you may suffer doubts and fears that have no basis of realism. But your doubts and fears are true if they exist in your mind; conversely, however, they're untrue if you deny their existence.

The point of all this, then, is: If you structure your thinking to where you believe you think only positive thoughts then you think positive thoughts because you believe you do. This is self-acceptance. And it minimizes your urge to justify yourself to others. And so once you learn to doubt yourself less, you're less afraid of others' criticism.

When you achieve this positive state of mind, you can realistically look at the facts, the conditions, that confront you. You'll be able to face up to being wrong if that's the case; and, right or wrong, you'll find yourself willing to share the job of doing things differently in the hope of discovering greater accord with others.

I suggest this method of overcoming your fears and doubts because I know it works.

Once you have the method working effectively for you, you achieve self-acceptance, a vital element to success. In the process of achieving self-acceptance you'll rid yourself of false beliefs—you'll no longer need them to justify your failures.

But let me emphasize here that what I term "positive thoughts" as distinct from "false beliefs" may not in themselves be true. False beliefs are negative, positive thoughts whether or not they're true, are beneficial.

William James, the nineteenth century American philosopher who developed the theory of pragmatism, suggested that certain beliefs are of great value to you even if they aren't necessarily true. The important thing for you, he said, was to believe them with sufficient intensity. He used this illustration:

You are, for instance, running away from a dangerous, man-eating tiger, and you run and run and finally come upon a wide crevice which you have to jump in order to escape the tiger. If you stop because you doubt you can make it, you would be devoured by the tiger. On the other hand, James said, if you believed you could make it, and took a couple of steps backward and got a running start and jumped for all you were worth—you still might not make it, and it would be no different from being eaten by the tiger. But you might make it and survive.

The point then is: If you believe you can do something you have a fighting chance of doing it. This is of vital importance to you. You may fail in your attempt, but that is a chance you must take. Otherwise, you'll remain frozen with doubt and fear. And you can't expect to enjoy life and expect to achieve much that way.

So, to sum up this chapter, let me re-emphasize my point: False beliefs, negative thinking, are based upon doubt and fear. And there is no realistic reason why you should be a victim of them.

If you have a choice between being wrong or being doubtful, choose to take the risk of being wrong. Your greatest danger, until you master positive thoughts, isn't that you'll do the wrong thing; it's that you'll do nothing.

The ability to reason, to think, is man's most tremendous possession, but if that doesn't point the way to action, it's worth little, if anything, to you. If you don't rid yourself of false beliefs and learn to act, all you have left is worry about whether it's safe, whether you're secure.

If, on the other hand, you act often enough, it becomes habitual. The habit of doing something about your problems can banish your doubts. And if you're willing to be wrong rather than doubtful, you've mastered positive thoughts and you're more than halfway toward your goal of success.

MILLIONAIRE SECRET #7

How to Start Small and Grow Big Fast in Your Own Business

There's a man in the small city of Oceanside, Calif., 40 miles north of San Diego, who's proved you don't have to live in a metropolitan city to build your way to success, happiness, and wealth. No matter where you live you can start small and grow big fast in your own business.

He's Eddie L. Robinson, a 6-feet, 175-pound, blue-eyed and brown-haired 46-year-old retired Marine Corps major.

What's so unusual about Major Robinson?

In 1964, he amassed the incredible record of selling $2 million in policies—an unheard of achievement for a first-year insurance agent who lived in a town of 40,000 persons. And each year since, he's been in the insuranceman's magic yearly "one-million-dollar-circle." That is, he sells more than $1 million of life insurance each and every year.

To achieve his success, Major Robinson reacted counter to the millions of men and women who each year leave small cities for metropolitan ones because they believe their hometowns offer them scant opportunity.

Major Robinson's success story proves, at least in his instance, that they could find success at home if they had the desire, ambition, and personal drive to go after it.

93

How and why has Major Robinson achieved such a large success in a small city? Has it simply been good luck?

Luck has had little to do with it.

Major Robinson, instead, has developed a personal success philosophy, and workable techniques, that if adopted by others would permit them too, to build successful careers in their hometowns.

Today, as well as continuing to personally sell more than $1 million of life insurance each year for the Massachusetts Mutual Life Insurance Company, Ed Robinson operates with his partner, Glenn E. McComas, a general insurance agency. His agency, the Karlsbad-Pacific Insurance, Inc., is in Carlsbad, a small city of 15,000 persons adjacent to Oceanside. Major Robinson has already begun to establish branches of his agency in even smaller towns in the region that surrounds Oceanside.

The keys to his success are these: the setting of realistic goals, personal drive, and an unrelenting ambition to be self-independent.

On a recent day, sitting in the office of his agency Major Robinson described his first goal, and the one he considers most important to both his personal and business life:

> I think that my most important personal and business achievement, based on my first major goal, was in making the transfer from a country boy with narrow viewpoints and not too much ability to really see how the other side lived, or the world for that matter, into what I like to consider myself today as a reasonably well-informed individual; one who has gained some educational background, both academic and from the school of hard knocks, in the number of years I've been an adult.
>
> To me it was a personal achievement and it seemed to be taking my plan (goal) a little higher than when I first established it.

He has never stopped setting goals for himself. Today, he said, his goal is to sell at least $1 million of life insurance each year.

"I've always had, since I've been in the insurance business, a goal from the very first day I came in," he said. "I want to sell over $1 million worth of insurance a year and I want to insure at least 100 lives each year."

His intermediate goal is "$25,000 a week, for $100,000 of insurance a month. Of course, this works out to provide $1 million production per year and 100 lives or more. You have to set a realistic goal; one that the individual can meet."

So far Major Robinson has met his goal each year. And his achievement has brought him a spacious home in an exclusive residential area, a Cadillac, and enough money to send his son through college.

> There have been weeks when I haven't sold $25,000, but there have been other weeks when I sold $75,000.
>
> I think the most important technique is to have a cast-iron ego, and by this I mean you shouldn't become 'down in the mouth' simply because someone has said 'no.' These things are just part of the occupation of confronting other people.

As for success techniques in his own profession, he believes they can be acquired.

"Understanding people, though, is more basic than any technique," Major Robinson said. "This means putting yourself in the other person's position, being nice, being courteous, having a pleasant and polite manner—that's the job of the salesman.

"Possibly the greatest technique there is in selling is simply getting out and selling," he added. "You have to see people, you have to constantly look for people; people are under every bush. All the people need is to be approached.

"I'm sure it's true elsewhere as it is in my area that the insurance business to be had hasn't even been scraped by the present insurance salemen. So, I know that I can make as much money as I can spread myself around.

"Now, as you expand your initiative and goal, " he continued, "your own technique can be polished to where it is more effective in bringing the people you find into a successful buying situation."

Robinson said he uses direct mail—sending out mail to potential clients and promising gifts, and making telephone calls, but, he said, "I've found for a long time that simply by circulating, going out and meeting and talking with people, and getting to know them, I do best. Once I've met them I ask them about their insurance program and present an idea that tantalizes them."

As Major Robinson puts it even more succinctly, you have to "get up and get" to achieve success in insurance as in any other occupation.

Put another way, Major Robinson simply makes the point: To succeed you must have an all-powerful desire (a goal), plan the steps toward achieving it, and then execute your plan.

What, for instance, does Robinson believe it takes to become a $1 million-a-year insurance agent?

"I believe if a person has the fundamental qualities to sell anything, he could certainly sell insurance as easily as he could refrigerators," he said. "I think selling life insurance, or any other intangible product is more difficult than selling a tangible one,. because you have to sell an idea and part the individual from his hard-earned money for something he may never himself see.

"I think if you have the basic fundamentals that are needed to sell: sincerity, belief in your product—knowledge of insurance can be acquired.

"I keep getting back though to the 'get up and get'. The ability to make things happen, the ability to have people to talk with and find people, and make every person you meet a potential client is also acquired; but it starts a long way back in basic initiative, the desire to get ahead, the desire to be more than what you are."

Robinson's sales philosophy obviously is to "get up and get." Reluctance to do this, he said, is the reason why many insurance agents as well as other businessmen fail.

There is no question in my mind that with all other things equal, that is, the ability of the individual to present himself successfully to another person, that if a person will see people, just see people and ask them to buy insurance, that he has to sell insurance.

It's impossible for him not to do so, but it's so easy for the young insurance agent and the newcomer, and also for the old guy who's been in the business for some time, to rationalize and say, 'I have got to get this letter written,' or 'I really must go down and get a new suit,' to put off putting himself in front of a client.

You simply can't sell insurance until you put yourself in front of a client and ask him to buy.

Major Robinson believes a major reason an insurance agent fails is because "He's not willing to work enough, he's not willing to train himself to work.

"The only reason, one of the only ones, for failure is that an awful lot of insurance agents come in with the idea that it is a wonderful business and I believe that deep down in their heart they're ashamed that they're selling something where they have to sort of sidle up to a guy and say, 'Hey, I have got something I have to peddle to you here' (like he was selling dirty pictures).

"I think the salesman has to be sincere, and I don't mean just superficially; he must really believe in life insurance. He must really believe that he's doing something for his client that no other person can do and, of course, his ability to do this is critical."

He also believes religious training and teachings can have a strong influence on a person's success or failure.

"The things religion stands for—treating all equally, being honest, having integrity, abiding by the rules and regulations— these are required for success because people can readily determine a phony and phony people don't play by the rules," he said.

"Most of the rules we abide by in our civilization today come under the general heading of religion; this is the controlling factor."

Perhaps the major reason Ed Robinson has achieved success is because of his overriding ambition to be self-independent—he believes the insurance business gives him that independence.

"I think everyone aspires to self-independence," he said, "but many people, unfortunately, aren't capable of living their lives independently; that is, without someone to tell them when to work, what the itinerary is, what the plan of the day is.

"The insurance business has given me the opportunity to decide these things for myself. I think any person who has the ability to regiment himself for other things, to control himself for doing things, and in organizing his time, has the talent to sell insurance.

"It's the profession for the person who finds the intangible is important," he said. "Who picks out people for their own salvation—very much like an evangelist. I'm not certain that maybe life insurance isn't a ministerial thing; you are carrying a message to people and performing an intangible service.

"I started out in my insurance career convinced that I could go out and find people and I could bring a message to them showing them I could help them, save them money, and help their families all at the same time."

Ed Robinson said the most effective way to sell insurance was to give the potential client "an idea."

He's able to do this because of his study of insurance methods and his preparation of plans. Such preparation permits him to come up with "an idea" tailor-made to each potential client's circumstances—income, family situation, other insurance, investments, and so on.

"I sell insurance 24 hours a day—it's not a part-time job with me," Robinson said. "In the beginning, I tried to see 20 persons a day. I don't have to see that many now; I see less people and my sales actually have gone up because my technique has improved."

What is his technique?

"The clients and prospects I see normally see me as an out-going individual relatively gay and carefree, well-dressed and apparently not working hard at the job This is the image I strive to maintain and promote, and I suspect other successfull insurance agents try to do the same thing."

But what the prospects don't know, and what Ed Robinson never dwells on, is the preparation he's made before he approaches a potential client.

"I try to have a general idea of all the terms, aspects and methods of insurance and investments and I try to know as much about as many things as I can," he said. "I feel I can at least hold my own if the guy pins me down on a specific question until I can get somewhere and find the answer. So far it's worked for me."

What, then, is Major Robinson's personal secret of selling?

"I suppose it's my ability to project myself, to control myself, to have empathy and to be attentive; but most of all, to get out and see people and ask them to buy my product," he said.

And what advice does he have for the young man just starting his career?

"I think the young man must accept that initially he's going to have some set-backs," Major Robinson said. "But he should target in on those worthwhile things he wants and then go after them through his own actions. He shouldn't dwell on all the things that 'might happen'—that's negative thinking and useless.

"I don't really believe that the ingredients for a successful life insurance man are really different from those for a successful engineer or successful race car driver. They boil down to the ability of the individual to comprehend, to think, to reason, have an agile mind, his ability to reason with other people and to put himself in their place.

"Especially as a salesman," he said, "he has to try and realize and design, even before the client does, what the client's thoughts are and then make those thoughts come out as the salesman wants them to. Every situation should try and be made to bear fruit in the direction you wish it to bear."

This, then is the technique Major Ed Robinson has used to win himself success. He believes it can work for others as well.

And he prefers to build his success in a small city; he enjoys the "atmosphere and the close personal relationships that can be developed." If you ask him: Does he regret not having built his career in a large city? "Not on your life," he replies. "For the man who wants to make it, and will work for it, there's as much opportunity today in America's small cities as there is in her large ones."

No one can dispute that Major Robinson speaks from a position of strength, achievement, happiness and unqualified success—all built for himself and his family in a small city.

So, the point based on Major Robinson's experience is that if you live in a small city and you believe you're stymied there, take another look at your situation. It's possible you, too, could find success in a small city, with these shortcuts that zoom your income.

MILLIONAIRE SECRET #8

How to Get Rich with Other People's Money

You control your destiny, but you do so only within the awful, inexorable framework of chance. A recklessly driven automobile swerves and the man in its path who might have been President and changed the destiny of a nation or even of the world is hurled instead into the unknown, endless eternity; another victim of the ever-present, waiting, and arbitrary hand of chance.

But in your quest for success, you don't concern yourself with chance; if you are to fall victim to its waiting arms, you must accept it. You do not, however, sit and wait for it to arrive.

Instead, while you can, and until chance comes, you do what is within your power to make the most of your life. And so, at some date in the future what will your answer be when you have to face the question: Did I commit myself to the struggle to make the most of myself? Will you be able to answer: I designed my life so that I was involved, absorbed, and enthusiastic; I did the very best I could, I have no regrets.

That, then, should be your life's pattern. And if at the moment it isn't, you snould start now to build a life for yourself that's involved, absorbed, and enthusiastic.

Let's look at a man who did. He's Dr. Wendell Phillips, explorer, archaeologist and developer of Middle East oil fields, who has plush offices in London and Switzerland and who today has a personal fortune that exceeds $100 million. From childhood he had an all-powerful desire to be an explorer; he never wavered in his goal.

After graduation from the University of California, with a degree in paleontology, Phillips joined the merchant marine and sailed to every theater of operations during World War II. His sea duty ended shortly after the invasion of Okinawa, when he became a victim of infantile paralysis. While convalescing he made a decision to lead an expedition to Africa—he set for himself a goal. He was 25 at the time and dead broke.

"I soon discovered, though, that an expedition was easy to conceive, but hard to deliver," he said. "No one wanted to take a young, inexperienced college graduate with no firsthand knowledge of Africa."

A lesser man at this point of discouragement would have quit, have given up his goal; he could have become a victim of fear—the fear he couldn't succeed, or he could have fallen prey to doubt—the doubt of his own ability. Instead, Phillips reasoned that what he needed to achieve his goal was the backing of a famous man. He went in search of one.

The late Field Marshall Jan Christian Smuts, Prime Minister of the Union of South Africa, was at the time representing his country at the United Nations in New York. Phillips hitch-hiked across the country to see him. Armed with only a letter of introduction from Robert Gordon Sproul, president of the University of California, Phillips persisted until Smuts agreed to see him. Once in Smuts's presence, Phillips talked so persuasively that he left with a letter stating that Smuts was honorary chairman of the expedition's advisory board. Within 10 days, Phillips had 10 new trucks, 50,000 gallons of gasoline, steamship transportation, electrical supplies, recording equipment, hundreds of thousands of dollars worth of other necessary gear, and operating funds. He was off to Africa.

Phillips now began a career of exploration and adventure that, with the help of other people's money, ultimately would make him famous and wealthy. After his initial African expedition, he formed the American Foundation for the Study of Man. Money became easier to obtain and soon scholars the world over began to recognize his archaelogical work in Aden and Egypt.

It was in Yemen, in 1952, that Phillips first attracted world-wide attention. One day he sat at his desk and wrote to Prince Abdullah, Foreign Minister of Yemen. In his letter he asked permission to excavate at Marib, the forbidden city, and the ancient capital of the Queen of Sheba.

Although many before Phillips had tried to obtain it, no one had ever been given permission to dig at Marib. But Phillip's persistence paid off. His letter to the foreign minister brought a reply that the King, Imam Ahmed, would like to see him. Once in the King's presence, Phillips talked so persuasively and enthusiastically that the King granted the young archaeologist the permission he sought.

Phillips, who believes success attracts more success, had barely finished the excavations at Marib when he received an invitiation from the Sultan, Said bin Taimur, to visit Oman. The Sultan agreed to permit Phillips to set up operations at Dhofar to explore and excavate for three years. All finds, were to be divided 50-50 between the Sultan and Phillips.

The American archaelogist made a series of valuable historical finds, but the biggest, and the one that set him on the road to riches, was the discovery the Sultan desperately wanted to tap the oil he believed was deposited somewhere in his land.

"If there's oil in Oman," Phillips, in effect, told the Sultan, "I'll find it for you."

Once again Phillips put to work his talent to sell himself and his ideas. The result was that the Sultan granted him the oil concession for Dhofar.

Dhofar, where Phillips and his staff were excavating, was 640 miles west of Muscat, a province with a coastline extending 200 miles. It contains 38,000 square miles, which was larger than all Portugal and about the size of Ohio.

Phillips now faced his greatest challenge. He knew he didn't have enough money to carry out such a vast exploration and oil drilling operation. Here again, at another critical point in his career, he could have allowed himself to become a victim of doubt, but Phillips never permits himself to think of failure. So, he decided he'd have to find some partners with money.

Quickly, he divided the 38,000 square miles into a thousand separate units, he tucked three-fourths of them away for himself and then set out to sell the remaining fourth. Within a few months, he'd sold the plots to oil companies for $1.5 million.

It wasn't long before the Sultan, and Phillips, had several oil gushers. The Sultan was so pleased he gave Phillips two offshore oil concessions. Phillips sold one of these to a West German combine, keeping five percent for himself. Later he also acquired the copper mining and commercial fishing rights in Oman.

The millions poured in and soon Phillips became by far the world's wealthiest archaeologist. He had his oil operations in Omar under control; it was time to develop and meet a new challenge. He found it in Libya. There King Idris gave him a franchise over 9,000 square miles in which to seek oil, and promising Phillips three percent royalties. Later Phillips transferred the franchise, but today he reportedly draws some $200,000 annually from oil production in Libya.

How much is Phillips worth today?

"I read the other day that I had $365 million," he said. "I don't really know the real figure, but offhand I'd say my Libyan holdings are worth at least that much."

Phillips, then, is a man who refused to fall victim to fear, self-doubt, or indecision. His refusal made him a multi-millionaire. Phillips knew what he wanted, he understood how to get the use of other people's money, he had an all-powerful desire and he took the action needed to meet and overcome the challenges that faced him as he sought his goal. You can, you must, do the same if you're to achieve real, lasting success.

Still another man who knew what he wanted, refused to become the victim of fear and doubt, and never veered from the path of his goal, is Richard B. Helms, 55-year-old Director of the U.S. Central Intelligence Agency (CIA). He's the first professional intelligence agent to rise through the ranks to the top of CIA.

Helms was born in a Philadelphia suburb in 1913, grew up in Orange, New Jersey, and spent two high school years in Switzerland and Germany with his father, a sales executive for Alcoa Aluminum, who had retired and had decided to live in Europe. He learned to speak fluent French and German and became a foreign correspondent for the United Press in Berlin on the eve of World War II.

Helms quickly showed his persuasiveness and aggressiveness when he obtained an exclusive interview with Adolf Hitler. On the other hand, he demonstrated what a practical man he was when he threw over the excitement of a correspondent's job in a Europe about to explode, and returned to the United States to manage advertising for the Indianapolis *Times* because it was a better job, though less glamourous.

If there's one characteristic that dominates Helm's make-up above all others, it's decisiveness. He never doubts himself and he refuses to take counsel of fear. And evidently it was because of these characteristics that he became a superb intelligence officer in the Office of Strategic Services during World War II. His contribution to the OSS was so outstanding that when the CIA was created in 1946, he became an assistant director, and throughout its history he's been either an assistant or deputy director.

Helm's decisiveness was demonstrated in 1962 when high government officials were insisting an invasion of Cuba to overthrow Fidel Castro's communist regime was both necessary and feasible. Helms said "no."

The report on the incident is that the late Robert F. Kennedy, then U.S. Attorney General and the closest man to the President, his brother John F. Kennedy, asked Helms his views as assistant director for CIA's Division of Plans. Helm's detailed analysis boiled down to this: Unless you use American aircraft and warships to completely support the invading refugees, and unless you provide them with modern arms and equipment, Castro's army will cut them to pieces.

The result of the Bay of Pigs fiasco is history. Helm's voice, one of the few raised against the invasion, was ignored. And the United States suffered its most shameful defeat of the Cold War.

The point, then, is this: Helms, as well as Phillips, are men of their own counsel. They've refused to permit themselves to become victims of fear, doubt, and indecisiveness. Instead, they rely on their own sound judgment, their good self-image, and their willingness to take a calculated risk.

Identical attributes can be applied to Bernard Cornfeld the 41-year-old head of Investors Overseas Services, Ltd., the Switzerland-based holding company for mutual funds, insurance companies, banks, and anything else that'll earn money. The actual value of the financial syndicate he runs has been conservatively put at half-a-billion dollars.

That isn't bad when you consider that Bernie Cornfeld launched with virtually nothing an operation that would eventually become an international financial empire. He started out in 1956 with a beat-up 1947 Chrysler, an empty billfold, a loosely formed idea—and an all-powerful desire backed up by his willingness to take a risk.

Twenty years ago few that knew him would have guessed Bernie Cornfeld would become a multi-millionaire before the age of 40. For in the post World War II years Cornfeld studied at Brooklyn College and earned a degree in psychology, a field some distance from finance and commerce. With his degree in hand he obtained a $300 a month job as a social worker in Philadelphia. But it didn't take him long to decide he was headed for a dead end career.

"I just decided that there were other, more lucrative ways to provide social services," Cornfeld today recalls.

He chucked his social welfare job and became a mutual fund salesman. Abruptly, almost overnight, he discovered he had a talent for salesmanship and by 1956 he'd put enough money aside to vacation in France. Europe appealed to him. So much so that he attempted to get his bosses at the Investor's Planning Corporation to let him stay on in France and set up a European sales operation. The bosses refused. So, Cornfeld resigned. Later he'd do business with his old company but their relationship would then be somewhat reversed.

Cornfeld now looked elsewhere for an opportunity that would permit him to live and work in Europe. He turned to the managers of the Dreyfus Fund and he quickly convinced them he had the know-how and could line up the manpower to expand their sales organization in Europe. Cornfeld began modestly; the two million Americans living in Europe were his sales target. And although he and his crew sold mutual fund shares like a water vendor at a peanut-eating contest, he discovered that because of currency restrictions he couldn't get the money out of France.

So Bernie Cornfeld packed, piled into his old Chrysler and headed for restriction-free Geneva, Switzerland. Here he expanded his sales organization. By 1960 he felt he was ready to establish his own mutual fund. He called it the International Investment Trust (IIT).

The IIT was simply the beginning for him. As it grew, Bernie Cornfeld began to build a complex organization of mutual funds, banking and insurance interests. By the mid-1960s his Investors Overseas Services owned or controlled 83 corporations. His sales force included 8,500 men and women in 100 countries.

Bernie Cornfeld had some setbacks in 1970-71 when there was a slump in the stock market. However, he wasn't hurt too badly. He's still estimated to have a personal fortune in the neighborhood óf $40 million. In 1971 he paid $500,000 for movie actor George Hamilton's 22-bedroom Hollywood mansion. Even with his reverses, Cornfeld still represents one of the great financial success stories of the twentieth century.

A business associate said one of Cornfeld's success secrets is, "He had an absolutely uncanny ability to rally really competent people around him and set their talents free."

That oversimplifies it. Bernie Cornfeld has much more than that going for him. He, for instance, is goal-oriented; he has the courage to act on his judgment, and he's always been willing to take the needed risks to achieve his goal.

These are the characteristics that made him a multi-millionaire. They, too, can help you achieve your own success. Adopt them and make them yours.

To conclude this chapter, let me repeat that you live in the inexorable framework of chance, but you needn't, you mustn't, depend on chance for success or failure. You cannot rely on chance, on "luck," and you can't base your life on the opinions of others. You must do it yourself, and you must do it in the world full of frustrations and dangers. You must, then, take your chance, and make it work for you.

MILLIONAIRE SECRET #9

How to Tap the Hidden Sources of Wealth in Your Family

Thus far the success techniques described apply equally to men and women. This chapter, however, is aimed primarily at women who seek success, although its contents also should be of interest to men because it reveals how to tap the amazing hidden sources of wealth that can be found in their families: the unused womanpower that is now being wasted.

But because of a woman's tri-role—wife, mother, and career girl—many times carried on simultaneously, I considered it best to devote this separate chapter to success techniques for women—those that can be adopted and applied in their roles as wife, mother, and career girl.

Let's begin by asserting that successful women, like successful men, are alert persons who listen intently when people talk; they observe people, businesses, and neighborhoods. This alertness serves to satisfy, in part, their hunger for knowledge about money, how to make their personal lives more successful, and how to discover business and career opportunities. And the successful woman sets her goal and keeps after it until she achieves it.

A few years ago, for instance, three women—Marian Knobler, Magda Bierman, and Dorothy Arden—built a women's apparel manufacturing firm from virtually nothing, starting with a $2,000 investment. Within nine years the firm's sales reached $2.5 million annually. When asked what accounted for their success, the three agreed, "It was because of our perseverance— we refused to give up even at those times when it looked as if we wouldn't make it."

So, the successful woman, as the successful man, must have an all-powerful desire and take the action and risks needed to achieve her goal.

But if you talk to women about their goals, as I have, you'll be startled at the result. I've found the typical American woman has no specific idea, most often not even a general idea, of what her life's goal is. She has no idea of her wealth wants or needs. She vaguely desires more money, a better car, a more comfortable home in which to live; but she doesn't know how much she really needs. Why? Because she's never taken the time to establish a specific, all-powerful goal for herself.

Frequently when I ask a woman what her goal in life is, she'll provide me general answers such as these: "I just want to be a good wife and mother;" or "I want to do everything I can to help my husband make his career a success," and so on.

These, as far as they go, are worthwhile goals, but they're too general.

On the other hand, the successful woman, whether it be in her role as wife, mother, or career girl, or all three, has specific goals such as these: "I intend to earn $5,000 within the next year so that our two children can attend a private school;" or "These are the steps I'll take to widen our social and business contacts within the next six months to further my husband's career as a lawyer."

So, the first thing the sucessful woman does, and what you must do if you're to achieve your own success, is determine a specific, all-powerful goal. When you've decided, write it down.

Then list the methods you plan to use and set a deadline for each intermediate step along the way to your major goal.

If in setting your goal you decide you can't achieve it because you haven't the needed education, because you're too busy looking after your husband and children, or because there aren't any opportunities, you're a victim of what I call the "loser's syndrome." Unless you switch such negative thinking, right now, into positive thoughts, you'll never achieve success—not even in the roles you may cherish the most, those of wife and mother.

Regardless of the odds, the difficulties, that face you, you can, if you have an all-powerful desire, overcome them.

Mrs. Wayne Quillin of Granada Hills, California, did and you'll agree that she faced an obstacle, and still does, that hopefully will never confront you.

Mrs. Quillin thought she was losing her mind when she began to feel tingling in her legs, saw double images, slurred her words and dropped her fork during dinner for no apparent reason.

"I even fell a couple of times, and I was afraid of dropping the baby every time I picked him up," said the mother of two boys. "I was told I had multiple sclerosis five years ago, and I cried for two days after that. When you realize there's no cure. . ."

Multiple sclerosis is a continuing disabling disease of the brain and spinal cord that causes paralysis and other disturbances of nerve impulses which control such bodily functions as walking, talking and seeing. Severe tremors and extreme weakness are common. It's a disease that usually gets progressively worse, will put many of its victims in wheelchairs and lasts a lifetime. Patients are often confronted with years of hopeless days. The cause, prevention and cure for the disease haven't yet been discovered.

Mrs. Quillin understandably could have permitted herself to lapse into deep depression, lose interest in her surroundings, and have resigned herself to a life of despair.

Instead, she decided to help others learn more about multiple sclerosis. She set her goal and acted. In 1968 she became president of the San Fernando Valley chapter of the Volunteers in Multiple Sclerosis. And today she works with such television stars as Carol Burnett in helping those afflicted with the disease to help themselves.

"I was lucky," Mrs. Quillin said. "My symptoms don't appear too often. And once a family learns more about multiple sclerosis and learns to live with it, things become much easier."

Mrs. Quillin helped her family, she helped others, and she helped herself to learn to live with the crippling disease. The result has been that she's achieved her goal of living a happy, useful life even though she's afflicted with a disease that would be unbearable to many another person.

So, when you consider your own circumstances and begin to feel that you're stymied, that you're hemmed in by family responsibilities, and such, think of Mrs. Quillin. If you do, you'll quickly realize that your problems, for the most part, are small ones.

The desire to live a happy, useful life, although afflicted by disease, enabled Mrs. Quillin to achieve her goal. It can work for you, too. Because, after all, desire is the starting point of all achievement.

But, you say, I'm a married woman with children; how can I achieve a goal of my own?

Well, the motion picture actress Marion McCargo Moses did it after four children and 15 years of marriage. And what was the ingredient that propelled her to success? It was, again, an all-powerful desire.

"The desire has to be deep enough to send you into action," Miss Moses said, "and you can't allow yourself to contemplate defeat. If you allow yourself to be flattened by rejection, you're finished. Some talented and capable people fail because they don't bounce back. Disappointments can be heartbreaking if you allow them to be.

"But success," she said, "must be defined in personal terms. It can't be judged by what others see, but what it gives you. True success is measured in happiness, not material reward."

Miss Moses insists her personal success formula is based upon four elements: (1) Desire, (2) Ability to accept rejection, (3) Concentration, and (4) Hard work.

"Another important factor," she said, "is relating to people. If you aren't pleasant to work with, if your ambition makes you an egotist, this will be a stumbling block. But while you are training, acquiring experience, and, in turn, confidence, you mustn't lose sight of the importance of your personal appearance."

The factor that all successful women, such as Marion Moses and the others, have in common is staying power. Each one has refused to quit; they've been willing to put in their apprenticeship, spend the time needed to learn what was necessary to achieve their goals.

Eugenia Sheppard, the nationally-known society-fashion newspaper columnist, is an example; she put in a long apprenticeship for her fame. Twenty years before she started her column, she'd come to New York from Columbus, Ohio, an ambitious divorcee, a graduate of Bryn Mawr College, and a former society editor of the Columbus *Dispatch.*

In New York, she worked on the *Women's Wear Daily,* then joined the now defunct New York *Herald Tribune* to report on home furnishings. Later she covered beauty, and still later, fashion.

Finally in 1956 she felt prepared to launch her nationally syndicated column. It quickly succeeded and Miss Sheppard today in her 60s is considered by her colleagues as an aggressive, goal-oriented reporter.

It was, then, Eugenia Sheppard's determination to achieve the goal she's set for herself, to have the staying power that enabled her to persist, and to act, when needed, that has gained for her fame, position, and money.

But, you say, I don't want to wait until late in life to achieve my goal! I want to achieve it now! So did the internationally-known fashion designer Betsey Johnson. She began the climb to her goal at age 21. She started as a moonlighting dressmaker for the editors of *Mademoiselle.* And while doing odd chores, she doodled original and clever fashion sketches on pads. One day she showed two of her sketches to a women's wear manufacturer.

The manufacturer liked her sketches, signed her to a contract, and put her to work designing. Within a year she was one of the hottest designers off New York's Seventh Avenue and a one-woman rival to some of the biggest fashion houses in the country.

One fashion writer has described Betsey Johnson this way:

> Betsy Johnson looks like anything but a fashion person. She
> is short and chubby with dark blond hair and the well-scrubbed
> demeanor of a 4-H girl who decided to become a beatnik.
> Nothing is too much or Mod for her to design or wear.

So, with her all-powerful desire, her willingness to act, and to work hard, Betsey Johnson quickly became the most prolific, and most successful, designer of radical pop fashion, as well as the spokesman for a generation of young women who demand something totally different from what their mothers asked for in clothes.

Miss Johnson wanted a huge success and she wanted it while she was still young; she got it as did petite and imaginative 25-year-old Linda Sinay of Los Angeles, the founder of Sinay & Associates, an advertising agency. She's one of the tiny tycoons—girls in their 20s who could have done less but dared to do more, putting themselves in the upper one percent of America's working women by earning more than $10,000 a year.

Linda Sinay is young, she had a goal, and she was willing to take a risk. These factors paid off for her in a big way. She thinks young, hires young (the average agency age is 24½) and focuses young on the youth market, where she is placing her business bet.

In five years her agency has grown from an at-home operation with no capital to billing $1 million a year, a respectable figure for a small ad agency. In addition, her salary has grown from zero to $25,000 a year by serving such accounts as Kirby Shoes, Tropic-Cal Sun Glasses, High Tide Swimwear, and Buffum's.

What's her success formula? She described it:

> I learned early I couldn't work for anybody. I had to do it myself. I still do. And I try to hire people just like that. There's no mystique. I'm not a witch. But I know if you have confidence, know who you are and work hard, you can make it. It's there to be had.

While Linda Sinay has achieved her success in advertising, a sunny, young, low-keyed blond named Jinx Kragen has begun to make her reputation as a writer. She, too, has used the elements of desire and action to achieve success.

Almost any day Jinx Kragen can be found typing on the patio of her comfortable home in Hollywood above the Sunset Strip.

With her former college roommate, Judy Perry, Jinx is the author of two best-selling cookbooks, *Saucepans and the Single Girl* and *The How to Keep Him (After You've Caught Him) Cookbook.*

It was staying power that enabled Jinx and Judy to sell their first book. Jinx said the two of them did everything wrong in writing their first book on speculation—it took them a year of their spare time—and then attempting to sell it on their own.

"We never got past the aged receptionist at one big publishing house," they said.

Finally, after it was accepted, they hired an agent. "I doubt if anyone could re-create those circumstances," they agreed.

But today Jinx Kragen is writing a television situation comedy based on the cookbooks, she helped write the "Pat Paulson for President" book, sold a television script, and has a screenplay in progress.

Okay, you say, this is fine for those of us who want to become career women, but my major goal in life is to be as successful as I can as a wife and mother. What about me?

Millions of women have combined a successful career with their other roles of wife and mother; others have combined their home roles with outside activities such as club work, charities, going to college, and so on. They've done it successfully even though more American marriages appear to be unhappy and in jeopardy than ever before. The oft-heard phrase, "people are getting married these days just to get a divorce," though seemingly a gross exaggeration, applies, unfortunately, to a good part of the United States.

The fact is, says Dr. George Macer, a recognized authority on marriage problems and a University of Southern California gynecologist-obstetrician, "the happily married couple seems to be an oddity." He has reason for this assumption. About one-third as many couples get divorced each year in the U.S. as get married. In Los Angeles County, where Dr. Macer practices, there were 73 divorces or permanent legal separations per year for every 100 marriages. This is three times the national average.

What's behind this crisis? Why can't couples make their marriages work?

One common reason is that either one or both of the marriage partners haven't the all-powerful desire to make the marriage succeed nor are they willing to do what is necessary, to act, to achieve a happy partnership that brings fulfillment to both partners.

It's because of this that I decided to include in this chapter, with the help of experts, some of the answers to how men and women can be more successful in marriage. It's for you if you're about to be married, if you're happily married and want to know how to be even happier, or if your marriage is in trouble and you want to know how to save it. I'll also discuss how parents can better understand their children and how a sound relationship with them can lead to a more fruitful marriage and a happier home life. That, admittedly, is a large goal, but the experts insist, that through study and research, they've uncovered some of the secrets that'll bring you a happier and more successful marriage and family life.

The crisis in marriage is affecting the stability of American society. Judge William E. McFaden, head of the Los Angeles Conciliation Courts, puts it even more bluntly: "It is not farfetched to say that the health and stability of family relationships is the most important single problem facing our society," he said. "Many social evils we attack and try to eradicate are symptoms of a deterioration of family responsibility." He believes one of the major problems of today's marriages is that too many couples weren't properly prepared for marriage in the first place. The experts agree you can read in advance the signs that two people have or haven't what it takes for a happy marriage.

These factors, the experts say, are the ones to look for: happy childhood of both mates, parents of both partners happily married; ability to get along with people and adjust to custom; wholesome sex attitudes; freedom from fear or prudery; a naturally happy disposition.

On the other hand, if you think, for instance, that you'd have a more successful marriage if you were better educated—forget it. Dr. Macer said education, in itself, has nothing whatever to do with being happily married. Just the opposite appears to be true.

"'Higher education' has certainly not taught the way to marital maturity; it seems that the higher the educational level, the more conflicts and tensions are present, with each partner blaming the other for the discord," he said.

Do most marriages in trouble need counseling by psychiatrists and marriage counselors? They don't in Dr Macer's judgment. "They (the married couples) basically know what or from where their conflicts arise," he said. "The majority of these couples can solve their own problems if they are given a tool by which to evaluate their marriage and in so doing learn to communicate."

Dr. Macer doesn't, however, downgrade the need for psychiatrists and marriage counselors in diagnosing and solving certain marriage problems. "Those that are more involved and go back into childhood insecurities and conflicts should not be handled in a cursory manner and should be referred to those with more time and experience," he said.

Mrs. Frances Margolin, a San Diego clinical psychologist and a Superior Court associate conciliation counselor, agrees with Dr. Macer that a breakdown in communication most often brings marital discord. "Our culture has created a communications barrier," she, in effect, said, "and in a successful marriage it must be broken down. The unspoken messages of love are the one way to break it down, but," she warned, "If you can't communicate in the kitchen, you can't communicate in the bedroom."

Dr. Macer insists marriage is a business, probably the biggest in the world, certainly the most widespread. "To treat it as a business an inventory must be made at regular intervals," he said. "The rougher and more frequent the marital squall then the more frequently should an inventory be taken. By inventory is meant the appraisal of all areas that affect the union."

How do you take such a marriage inventory? Dr. Macer said you start by evaluating your own personalities. "You can tell him about the things that he does that irritate you and after you get through 'cutting him up' he does the same for you," he said. "No matter how insignificant you may feel the irritant to be, it should be mentioned. At first you may feel that you love him so that you shouldn't bring up the fact that he may be using that 'greasy kid stuff' or similar childish things—even the way he combs his hair or not brushing his teeth."

Dr. Macer insists, however, that a woman shouldn't use her physiologic periods of depression or tension or the minor ills of pregnancy as a means of getting sympathy or attention. He said he believes the success or failure of a marriage "really lies in the hands (or lap) of the female. A man is no more than a overgrown boy and that most girls, if they do it properly, can wrap them around their little, fingers. In most successful marriages this has been done very unobstrusively and the male has been made to feel that he has made all the decisions, when in reality the wife asks his advice then goes right ahead and does what she thinks is best, and it usually is."

Dr. Macer said the second item in his marriage inventory was finances. He advocates a "solid program of financial planning . . . the problems of budget are peculiar to each couple and should be arranged according to their own program."

The choice of friends, the third inventory item, is an important element of a happy marriage. "Don't be too intimate with couples who are unhappy in their own marriages," Dr. Macer said. "Don't listen to the marital problems of your girl friends, and above all, don't trust your closest girl friend; especially if she's unhappy in her own marriage and seeking solace in your home. We have seen more happy marriages broken up by an unhappy, conniving female that is on the prowl."

As for family interference, Dr. Macer said, "the couple's parents should be gently and firmly informed that the young couple is going to manage its own affairs and solve its own problems."

Dr. Macer places sex last on his marriage inventory list.

> There is no such thing as sexual incompatibility; that is just a reflection of personality or emotional incompatibily. I've never seen a couple who are incompatible sexually. Any happy couple can make a go of sex once they learn to relate in the marriage bed and enjoy the most intimate of relationships.

Your marriage is more in danger of failing between the fifth and seventh year and then again at the 20th year than any other times in your married life.

Why is this so? Dr. Macer said it's because of several reasons. "When you reach the fifth year of marriage," he said, "you know each other fairly intimately. Sex has become rather routine; probably there are two or three little ones around the house and, what with housekeeping and marketing your time and energy are pretty well taken up.

"In fact, they may be so taken up that you forget about that dominant, sexual male. He may begin to feel that there seems to be no time or affection left over for him. He begins to feel unneeded and unnecessary. He may soon begin to spend more nights out with the boys or even a girl."

By this time, based on Dr. Macer's observations, the wife may have let herself go; not taking time to have her hair done often; perhaps she's added a few pounds. The husband begins to be taken for granted. These are the danger signs and married couples should recognize them. What, then, can you do to recapture romance and bring new vitality into your marriage?

"It's my advice," said Dr. Macer, "that you plan one weekend out of four or six to get away together. Renew your affection, rediscover each other. This is essential in preventing the so-called 'tired-mother syndrome' or the development of 'cabin fever'."

Once this fifth-to-seventh year obstacle has been hurdled, a couple's marriage usually won't hit another stumbling block until about the 20th year. This is when, Dr. Macer said, "many a partner is suddenly told that their mate has had enough and now that the family responsibilities are less they would like to terminate the relationship. Such a situation would not have developed if throughout the years of marriage inventory hadn't been neglected. Communications broke down because you didn't find time for yourselves. You didn't resolve the little irritations that gradually explode after 20 years."

In the judgment of still another marriage expert, Dr. Beverly T. Mead, an Omaha, Nebraska, psychiatrist, these irritations could have been easily resolved over the years through an occasional good quarrel. He believes that if you have an urge to quarrel with your husband, go ahead—it's an indication of happy marriage.

"It's fair for the husband to pick a fight with the wife, too," Dr. Mead said. "Usually the misunderstandings the couple have can't be worked out unless there is conflict. But it's important to set ground rules for your fighting." Dr. Mead suggests these rules: (1) Don't belittle your spouse and don't disparage your husband's masculinity or your wife's femininity, (2) Fight in private, (3) Don't expect a settlement, (4) Don't allow your fight to develop into a grudge match, and (5) Don't go to bed angry.

So, to get to the basic problem and clear the emotional air, Dr. Mead said, a husband and wife should freely vent their emotions and concerns without planning to agree on anything. In other words, the argument is the best thing, not any solution that you may derive from it.

Dr. Macer has a list of "do's" and "don'ts" to help couples handle their problems. Three of them—don't go to bed angry, don't discuss your problem in public, and don't shout or swear at each other—agree with those of Dr. Mead. The others are:

Make it a habit to say 'please,' 'thank you,' I'm sorry,' and 'I love you.'

Don't do bathroom chores while your mate is using the bathroom.

Do remember dates, birthdays, anniversaries, etc.

Don't discuss your mate's sexual ability or inability with others.

Do be fastitious; go to bed clean.

Don't sell sex as a commodity to gain your way. This puts you in the class of the professional.

Do keep your bed interesting. Wear a nightgown one night,

pajamas another, nothing the next; tops one night, bottoms another. Have a couple of drinks and go to bed or go to bed and then have a couple of drinks or get up and scramble some eggs. Do anything to change the pattern.

Don't discuss your personal ills or defects, especially sexual, because each partner likes to think he has married something special.

These, then, are some of the proven methods, based upon years of research by experts, that'll enable you to have a happier, more successful relationship in marriage; but how do you succeed when you have the additional element of children?

Children can be the most agreeable or the most disagreeable product of marriage.

Dr. William E. Finch, a consulting psychiatrist of La Jolla, California, said the two most frequent quarrels between married couples are caused by questions of "how to spend money and how to raise children."

A psychologist, Mrs. Frances Margolin, said that since this is so, men, before they marry, should ask themselves; "Do I really want the whole package?" The whole package includes children and being able to support them.

"A woman will resent her husband if she wants children and he uses contraceptives to keep her from having them," Mrs. Margolin said, "and also if she has children and then has to work to be able to support them."

The experts generally agree that the problem is simply one of communication when it comes to relationships between married couples and also between them and their children. If you want to better communicate with your children and your husband and increase your understanding of them you should encourage them to "sound off."

Do this even if you don't like what they're saying or agree with it. The technique will help you eliminate the "generation gap" between you and your children and establish a sounder relationship between you and your husband.

In other words, the key to happy family life is better communication between and among all members of the family unit. This is the advice of a psychologist who has made a detailed study of parent-child communication.

The psychologist, Dr. Ralph Eckert, coordinator of counseling and guidance for Riverside, California, County public schools, also believes wives should encourage their husbands to talk, The best method to accomplish this is to ask interested questions and then listen attentively to the answers.

"The listening is as important as the questions," Dr. Eckert said. "The non-communicative man will respond to a truly interested listener." He said women usually don't need to be encouraged to talk, but that if they do, the same techniques are effective.

It's generally conceded that today's parents are stuck with the "generation gap."

Dr. Eckert believes that what causes much of this "gap" is the refusal of children to talk in the presence of their parents. This is why parents should encourage their children to talk with them. "Most young people won't tell their parents what they're really thinking because they are certain their parents will not accept or approve of their ideas," he said.

Probably the worst thing that can be done in a parent-child or husband-wife relationship, Dr. Eckert believes, is for one party to walk from the room in the midst of a talk and slam the door on further communication. Dr. Eckert said, in his judgment, there are seven common blocks to communication between parent and child and husband and wife. They are:

    1. The old-fashioned cross examination, the FBI technique. "It reveals your own distrust of the other person and is extremely damaging to his self-image."

    2. Evaluation. That is, don't say to a child or a husband, "You shouldn't have done that." Instead, ask in a question form, "Wouldn't it have been better if . . .?"

    3. Advice. Don't say, "If I were you." Say instead, "Have you ever considered . . .?"

4. Teaching. If you say to a child, "Do it this way," you may find what you want done isn't being done at all. Instead, teach by example.

5. Analysis. Both husbands and children resent being analyzed. Therefore, never use such phrases as, "The trouble with you is . . ."

6. Warnings. They're all right, but they should be phrased as questions, which will lead to an intelligent decision about the wisdom of the situation.

7. Reassurances. It's pointless to say, "Don't worry" to someone who is "sick about something." Say, instead, "What bothers you most about this?" After the problem has been talked out, then give "a little intelligent reinforcement."

One final point for wives from Dr. George Macer: "So if he (your husband) should come home in the evening growling like a bear, order the children around and make life miserable for you, just remember that he is probably passing down some of the frustrations of the day. He is just taking it out on his family which happens to be the most readily available object.

"A little patience, understanding, and ego-inflation will usually work wonders in calming the storm," Dr. Macer said.

What it all comes down to is this: It is through patience, compassion, understanding, forbearance and male ego-building by women that marriages and families grow into happiness.

Let's admit that life of a woman in her tri-role is more complex than that of the man. By tradition and culture her roles have been somewhat more solidified than that of men. Perhaps it is because of this that it takes more staying power, more imagination and creativity, and more compassion on her part to make a success of her life than it does the man.

But if she has all-powerful desire and is willing to take calculated risks, she can achieve success—great success—in whatever role of her three major ones she chooses, or in all three if that is her goal. And such a woman is the greatest "hidden source of wealth" any family can have.

MILLIONAIRE SECRET#10

How to Take Advantage of the Sex Factor in Business Dealings

In the unlikely event an international congress of self-made millionairesses should assemble to proclaim a queen, Laurie Hermanson Hancock might not win the crown, but she certainly would be dubbed the chief lady-in-waiting.

She's a self-made millionairess who'll tell you, if you ask, how you, too, can make a million dollars.

When I interviewed her she was the president of four southern California companies and the vice-president of a fifth in Trenton, New Jersey. She has reached this pinnacle of success in 25 years with nothing more than a high school education and a start in the workaday world as a part-time secretary to a small town high school principal.

Along the way though in her climb to success, Laurie (Mrs. John) Hancock has accumulated more than a million dollars in personal wealth and a salary she modestly estimated "in excess of $25,000 annually."

She doesn't hesitate to share the secrets of how she did it.

What distinguishes Laurie Hancock from other business-women success stories is that she believes any young woman, if she wants to badly enough, can, like her, start from scratch and achieve wealth and success.

"Yes, I believe any young woman of today can start from scratch and achieve wealth and success," she said. "There is no limitation on ingenuity and inventiveness, and new fields of endeavor are opening for women at an accelerated rate. Our technological changes in the last 20 years stagger one's comprehension—surely women will contribute much to the future as their acceptance in all areas of government and business grows."

Mrs. Hancock readily admits that an all-powerful desire to achieve a specific goal and the willingness to take the necessary risks are two essential ingredients for anyone, man or woman, who has an ambition to be wealthy.

What makes Laurie Hancock's achievement even more remarkable than most is that in the midst of amassing a fortune, she's been a successful wife and mother. With her husband, John, she's raised a family of four children.

And although it's doubtful if she'd admit it, Mrs. Hancock is a feminine dynamo—when she isn't working, she's developing business plans and strategy in her mind. It's a technique she's used all her adult life.

Mrs. Hancock, the daughter of an immigrant farmer from Norway, has, in fact, dedicated her life to achieving success as both a human being and a businesswoman. On both counts, she's a winner.

If you were to meet her in person, you'd confront an attractive 45-year-old woman, who's 5-feet 5-inches tall, weighs 128 pounds, and has blue eyes. Her hair is reddish-brown and, she said, "some people have complimentarily referred to it as the color of redwood." One of her companies manufactures Redwood outdoor furniture.

In the climb toward her goal, Mrs. Hancock has believed strongly in the ability of her mind to conceive and achieve. She's always been willing to go "the extra mile" in whatever she attempted. And she has constantly qualified herself for the next step upward and the steps beyond.

It's been a winner's philosophy for her. Today she has most anything she wants. She lives with her family in a $75,000 brick Georgian home with white columns that sits on a half-acre in Chula Vista, California, a city adjacent to National City where her plants are located. In the backyard tastefully arranged is at least one piece of every style of redwood furniture ever produced by her company.

She insists her obligations to her home and work haven't come into conflict.

"How do I manage to raise a family and still direct a large business?" she said. "It isn't easy. But when one is faced with the necessity, one manages to summon the courage and strength to do both, with God's help. I do try to budget my time so that I can spend some time with each child each day, except when I'm traveling, of course. Because I am the co-owner of the business, I do reserve the right to set my schedule so that their needs are met first.

"My thinking and planning for business isn't necessarily at a standstill during this time—nor is it confined to set hours of a day or days of the week," she said. "Aside from that, it is essential to have competent help at home—I would have no peace of mind without that. All in all, I feel it is important to train children to be independent and resourceful—and that parents shouldn't try to do everything for their children, as this doesn't allow them to mature naturally."

Laurie Hancock, who was raised on a farm near Thief River Falls, Minnesota, believes three major "breaks" were responsible for her success:

"First, being selected the outstanding business student in high school and having the opportunity to work as secretary to the principal after school and on Saturdays," she recounted. "Because it was financially impossible for me to attend college, this early training helped me to recognize that I had a natural aptitude for business and found it a stimulating challenge."

Her second "break," she believes, resulted from her work as a secretary to the president of the Union State Bank in Thief

River Falls for two-and-a-half years, and then as secretary to an aircraft corporation executive vice president in San Diego, California, for six years.

"I learned a great deal from each man as I saw problems and situations through his eyes and the psychology with which he dealt with them," she said. "Working for and with men of this caliber, I feel, was the second 'break' in my life because I learned so much from them; it was, in fact, an 'on-the-job' college education.

"My third 'break' was marrying John Hancock, a wonderful man with whom I've shared not only years of happy marriage, raising four children, and having a satisfying home life, but also sharing the challenge of building a family-owned business.

"He (John Hancock) has been the true 'builder' of the business and I do want him to have full credit for it," she said.

Laurie Hancock believes, as a human being, that each person should give back something to the world in which he lives. She's practicing this principle by founding and becoming a major benefactress of a new, independent, co-educational academy serving grades seven through 12. She hopes the academy budgeted at a cost of $6.5 million ultimately will have 400 students who represent all 50 states as well as the 29 states of Mexico and the Territory of Baja California.

Named the Santa Maria International Academy, Laurie Hancock said it would have "representative students from other countries of the world who would be assisted by a substantial scholarship program to permit them to live in American homes and to attend a secondary school whose aim of establishing the Brotherhood of Man and the Fatherhood of God would be an integral part of this educational institution.

I have a deep sense of responsibility toward the future of the community in which I live and the larger community of world relationships. I feel that the most important contribution I can make toward the future is to establish an educational institution to incorporate our best traditions, challenge excellence of academic pursuits and leadership, and to promote understanding and good will in a Christian atmosphere among the student body comprised of students from all countries of the world. I feel we will be developing a student body whose impact upon the relationship between countries would have profound effect in fostering future world peace.

Religion, then, is the center of Laurie Hancock's life and, she said, "I believe it gives meaning and balance to all of life. I believe true religion is expressed by what we practice in our daily lives—not only by attendence at Church on Sunday—and that our daily conduct in the business world, as in any other facet of life, expresses more eloquently our religious convictions.

"Specifically," she said, "this means having the highest business principles, honesty and fairness in all our dealings, and concern for every individual as a person. In our relatively small family-owned business, we try to treat all our employees with respect for their well-being as individuals on a team; by providing the best working conditions; by providing health and accident insurance for them and their families; paying the highest union scale; and helping them when problems arise."

There are some who believe Laurie Hancock isn't quite as altruistic as she would prefer her public image to portray.

She admits, herself, to having many human faults.

"My major shortcoming is being a perfectionist and I'm impatient with people, including my children, in this respect," she said.

There are employees of hers who say the lash of her tongue can be as painful as the sting of a whip.

It's obvious, however, that Laurie Hancock wants to create a good public image of herself and through it increase the business of her companies.

To help her do this, for instance, she retained the services of one of the West Coast's most successful, and effective, public relations counsels, William D. Nietfeld, of San Diego, a graduate of the University of Southern California and a former CBS network reporter. He developed and executed a nationwide public relations program for her.

Even though she lacks a college education, Laurie Hancock firmly endorses a higher education for young persons who want to make business their career.

"In 1941," she said about the date when she began her own business career, "it was possible to obtain employment with only a high school education, but this is becoming more and more difficult. I believe a woman should first get as much education as possible, including college, because competition is demanding it. I do believe, however, that all of life is a 'learning process' and should never stop with a formal education at any level. College is important, I believe, because it broadens one's horizons and helps an individual to achieve a more mature approach to life."

What, for instance, does Mrs. Hancock expect in this regard from her own children?

> I hope very much they will have the best education possible, including college, in order to meet the challenges of our future role in the world. Aside from that, I only wish that each one have a sense of 'purpose' in life and fulfillment of that role.

In other words, she wants them to have an all-powerful desire (goal) in life and be willing to do whatever is necessary to achieve it.

And although she knows that general knowledge is important to her children, as anyone else, in helping them reach their goal, she also knows that knowledge won't attract money unless it's organized into definite plans of action and directed to a definite goal. Lack of understanding on this point has led millions to falsely believe that "knowledge is power." It's nothing of the sort, it's simply potential power; it becomes real power when it's organized and directed toward a specific goal.

Laurie Hancock believes in helping young women to understand this principle when she gives them advice, based on her own experience and success:

"The best advice I could offer a young woman who wants to enter the business world and become a success is: (1) Be sure it's the career she wants and that she has some natural aptitude for it, (2) Be as well prepared educationally as is possible, and (3) Be willing to work hard.

"From there on," she said, "it's up to the individual as she's willing to use initiative, assume responsibility, and effectively discharge duties."

She also believes that leadership is an important element for success. Her own leadership technique, she said, was to expect the best of each individual, "it usually produces the best results.

"As far as I'm concerned, there's dignity in all work—and each employee, regardless of his position, whether janitor or president, has an important part in determining the success of a company. Success in business does mean a profit, of course, but there are other considerations such as having the best product at the most competitive price, pride in workmanship, and reputation."

This attitude toward leadership has worked for her, and Laurie Hancock believes it to be basically sound. And since she rose from a part-time secretary to the head of a group of multi-million dollar companies, she also has ideas on how a person can advance himself.

"To achieve promotions in a business firm," she said, "I certainly think 'attitude' is an important ingredient. To have the right attitude toward starting at the bottom, or any given place, learning the job and working up by contributing to the job rather than having the attitude of what the firm 'owes' the individual, is basic. This includes being willing to 'do a day's work for a day's pay.' Promotions come as a result of the 'extra' initiative and effort one is willing to expend."

A question frequently asked Laurie Hancock is: Do you find

it particularly difficult to compete and operate in a business world comprised mostly of men?

"I don't," she said. "For one thing, the field of home furnishings is a 'natural' for women—and a very interesting one as well. It's a field in which a woman can contribute her innate sense of style and functional design ideas. Sex isn't a plus or minus factor in business dealings; it's the ability to do the job. Barriers to women in business are disappearing as they prove themselves capable of handling professional and administrative duties."

Thus, the best way for a woman to take advantage of the sex factor in business dealings is to find a field where her natural feelings for style and design will help her rise more swiftly to the top.

Laurie Hancock is a champion of the independent businessman. She believes the person who wants to make a fortune would most likely do so by operating his own business or industry, large or small.

"In my judgment," she said as she summed up her philosophy, "those persons who have great faith in themselves, their product, and the courage to risk everything to achieve success work best for themselves. Independence has great rewards—it also has great challenges."

Why, you now ask, have I used this chapter to recount the success story of Laurie Hancock? That's easy. It's the true story of a real-life person who's achieved the success you seek. The methods she used may be adaptable to your own life, your own circumstances. So, study them, then adopt them. They worked for Laurie Hancock; they could work for you.

MILLIONAIRE SECRET #11

How to Develop the Millionaire's Point of View toward Money, Profit, Power and Success

Leonardo da Vinci said, "The life that is well spent is a long life." When he spoke those words he uttered a universal truth. It's one I'm sure you'll agree with; who wouldn't? But, of course, the question is: How do you determine, how do you achieve, a life for yourself that you consider well spent?

The answer: Develop for yourself a personal philosophy to live by, one that'll enable you to see for yourself, others and your surroundings in as realistic a fashion as possible. In other words, create your own personal philosophy—a "millionaire's point of view," so to speak—by which to guide your life and, therefore, preserve yourself as a functioning, productive, fully your life and, therefore, preserve yourself as a functioning, productive, fully alive, human being.

In doing the research for this book, I found a personal philosophy to be an essential characteristic of every successful man and woman I interviewed. It's one of the most dominant features of their lives.

141

And if you were to ask me what I found to be the common key to their "millionaire's point of view," I'd have to answer: Participation; through it they've verified their existence and made it real. By participation I mean being active, being involved, doing things, being stimulated and constantly alive to the persons and events that surround you.

These successful men and women have discovered for themselves that the person who doesn't participate, who's unconnected to his society, others, and his future, is an unalive person. Such a non-participant person is, in effect, alienated; he's a man out of rhythm with the world; he denies his existence as a human being.

The participating man, then is a unit of two: (1) His goal; and (2) His action to achieve his goal.

And let me emphasize here that the mind of the participating man functions well regardless of measured intelligence or education; that is, it functions well within its capacity to function. So, the mind of the highly-educated participating man functions better than the mind of an equally educated non-participant.

It is the participating man who knows failures, pain, and disappointment. And because he knows them he's spared emotional illness in times of stress and crisis. The so-called neurotic, for instance, is the person who has been to a large extent spared from the full force of failure, disappointment, and humiliation.

Psychiatrists and psychologists, using a vast body of study as their evidence, insist that man is born alienated and only through enormous effort accomplishes participation. If this is true, and I believe it, then you have the power to alter your nature and become a successful, participating human being.

The alteration of your nature comes through the development of your own personal philosophy; how you look at life, what values you establish for yourself and adhere to, how you view the people and the world around you, what you've decided you want out of life, and what you believe to be your responsibilities toward yourself, others, and your surroundings.

I don't intend, nor should anyone attempt, to give you here a personal philosophy you can adopt as a package. It wouldn't work because your personal philosophy must be based upon your own individual background, your culture, your education, your religion, and so forth. What I hope to do is simply show you that path to formulating a "millionaire's point of view" that will assist you in preserving yourself unto yourself so that you can build from it a happy, productive, and successful life.

Let's, for a start, look at some basic beliefs in the philosophies of successful men. They are: (1) Every conscious act has an incentive or motive, (2) To a healthy man inaction is the greatest of offenses, (3) A man determines his own destiny through his own efforts, (4) A man must develop to the fullest extent possible his capacity to participate with others and in the world that surrounds him, (5) A man has the ability to alter his nature if he has a strong enough desire to do so, and (6) If a man has the desire and is willing to take the risks to achieve his goal he'll succeed.

These are only some of the beliefs subscribed to by successful men. Again, neither they nor I can devise a personal philosophy for you; you'll have to create that on your own.

But one major warning: Adopt a philosophy based upon your own beliefs and learning; not those of others. There are devious, effective, practical men who combine their thoughts and practices and then set out to convince others that their philosophies are the ones all men should adopt and live by. The thoughts of these practical men are about their own advantage; and so are their practices. They usually dominate the actual situation in which they're involved; for instance, corporation president, publisher, influential politician, and so on. They, because it's to their advantage, encourage routine in others, and they also subsidize such thought and learning that doesn't interfere with their objectives; this they call sustaining the standard of the ideal. In the promotion of their self-interest they praise team-spirit, conformity, loyalty, devotion, obedience, hard work, and law-and-order. These practical men, however, temper their respect for the law—meaning the order of the existing status—on the part of others with most skilful and thoughtful manipulation of it in behalf of their own self-serving ends.

These men denounce as subversive any signs of independent thought on the part of others that might disturb the conditions that give them profit and power. They tend to think only of themselves; they convince themselves that what they believe is right is right for everyone else.

Don't, I warn you, let yourself become a victim of these practical, self-serving men. Don't let them make their personal philosophy your philosophy. These men are only able to direct the thoughts of others because all too many men find the task of independent thought difficult, worrisome, and frustrating. There are all too many who prefer to be told what to do, what to think, rather than making decisions for themselves. They are the followers, and they admire those who'll do their thinking for them.

This is why symbols such as a metal to denote military rank, labels that brand such as "socialist, fellow-traveler, communist, conservative and liberal," and cliche slogans such as "the early bird catches the worm," have been so readily accepted by so many tens of millions of people—the non-thinkers, the non-questioners.

When a man, for instance, tells you, "all trade unionism is socialistic therefore its bad for you and your country," ask yourself this question: How are his ends served by attempting to get me to adopt the same opinion? Frequently, as you know, it's simply because he doesn't want to pay higher taxes even though he can well afford to. And when another man tells you, "You shouldn't change jobs because you'll get a reputation as a job-jumper and that's bad for your career," what he may actually be concerned about is that to replace you will cost him more money than he's currently paying you.

The motives of men vary and constantly change; if you are to succeed you need to learn to understand them as best you can—you can only do this as a thinking, questioning person.

So, let me emphasize, the willingness to engage in independent thought enables you to escape the clutch of custom and gives you the opportunity to do old things in new ways, to be creative, and to construct new ends and new means. There is an alternative to nearly every problem and situation that confronts you. To discover and define this alternative, then, is the task of the mind through observing, remembering, contrasting, contriving, and creating.

If you can learn to ignore the limitations of your environment, to throw off the cliches, the slogans, and the symbols, then you can become an independent thinker who'll use your own power and use it to devise new ways of doing things.

And if you'll apply this same principle when you construct and adopt your own personal philosophy, you'll have built for yourself a mental foundation that no one can destroy.

It is such a mental, philosophical, foundation that enables you to "preserve yourself." It will be so strong, and so constructed, that you'll be able to preserve yourself under all conditions of stress and crisis.

Let's, briefly, look at a man who's philosophy sustained him against almost insurmountable odds.

The man, U.S. Navy Rear Admiral Edwin W. Rosenberg, refused to believe the doctors in 1945 when they told him he would die of cancer. In late 1968, very much alive, he assumed command of the Seventh Fleet Amphibious Force in South Vietnam.

Rosenberg, a 1942 U.S. Naval Academy graduate, was invalided out of the Navy in 1945 when medical officers found cancer after his return from World War II duty as a navigator on an aircraft carrier. Between 1946 and 1950 he survived four bouts with cancer even after doctors who found a growth on his kidney told him, "You've got two weeks to live." Rosenberg refused to accept the verdict.

"Let's get started with the X-ray treatment," he told doctors at Chelsea Naval Hospital in Boston. The X-rays worked and the cancer was burned out.

His life saved, Rosenberg set about saving his career. He believed in himself, he had a personal philosophy that gave him inner courage. As a result he twice convinced the Navy Retirement Board that he was cured. However, each time the doctors found another cancer, in the groin for the second time and in the neck.

But Rosenberg, who from his boyhood in Sarpy County, Nebraska, had had an all-powerful goal of becoming a naval officer, refused to give up. He continued with the X-ray treatments and kept fighting to get back into uniform.

Rosenberg never waivered either in his philosophy or his goal. By September, 1948, he had convinced the Navy he should be given temporary duty as an instructor at the Naval Academy. This was progress, but he was still on the retired list—he wanted off.

Again he asked the Navy to return him to full active status. "Not a chance," he was told. "It'll take an act of Congress."

"If that's what it takes, I'll get it," Rosenberg responded.

Senator Bourke B. Hickenlooper of Iowa introduced the special measure and in September, 1950, President Harry S. Truman signed it. Then in 1952 Rosenberg took command of his first ship, the destroyer *J. Douglas Blackwood.* At the time he held the rank of commander; since then he has gone through the rank of captain and been promoted to rear admiral.

Rosenberg succeeded because he refused to live by the limitations imposed by others—the rules and regulations of the Navy that said he couldn't be returned to active duty. And he did something to have them changed; and he succeeded.

The point is this: There are various ways in which your world can be construed. Some are undoubtedly better than others. Admiral Rosenberg construed his world one way, the men who opposed his goal construed it another.

If your personal philosophy is valid you'll know that whatever confronts you is subject to revision, modification, or replacement. This is basic, it's what makes for progress. So you must believe there are always alternative avenues available to choose among in dealing with others and with your surroundings. You needn't paint yourself into a corner; you needn't be completely hemmed in by circumstances; you needn't become the victim of your past.

Acceptance of these alternatives represents a philosophical point of view. As I stated earlier, I haven't any intention of attempting to create for you a complete philosophical system— that's your job. What I'm trying to do is set out for you a starting point from which you can build.

And as you think through, and analyze, the construction of your personal philosophy, you'll undoubtedly come face to face with the centuries old question: Do men make events, or do events make men?

I believe "men make events."

Let's use an example: Suppose you're to cut a cake. There are an infinite number of ways of going about it, all germain to the task. If the cake is frozen, some of your usual ways may not work—but you can still do it using a variety of methods. But let's suppose the cake is on the table and guests are present. Certain limiting factors have been set up about how the meal is to be served.

The cake is considered part of the meal. There are social conventions about serving wedge-shaped slices with the point always turned toward the diner. If you accept these conventions, you'll find your course of behavior determined, fixed, and little latitude left to you. You aren't the victim of the cake, but rather of your notions of etiquette under which the cake has been cut and served.

But let's further suppose that the cake makes you ill. Aren't you then a victim of circumstances? Of course, I might ask why you ate it in the first place? I could even suggest your illness needn't rob you of your freedom; it might increase your scope of action because of the tolerance and sympathy that would be shown you by others.

So, the point it this: You subordinated your freedom—the method you might have liked to use to cut the cake—to preconditioned ideas about etiquette. The cutting of the cake itself didn't limit your freedom; therefore, you could have, if you hadn't been bound by custom, cut the cake any way you wanted, so that you could have determined the event instead of permitting the event to determine your action.

If you think of your actions in a similar context you'll soon begin to realize that most of what you do is determined by someone else, by custom, by preconceived ideas; but it doesn't have to be that way if you don't want it to be. In other words, grasp control of your own actions—your own destiny.

Now we come down to the fact that thinking, and action, by an emotionally mature person is dominated by reality rather than by wishing. And your philosophy also must be dominated by reality.

The thinking person also has a certain amount of insight; that is, he sees himself with reasonable objectivity. He knows he isn't perfect; he makes errors in his appraisal of himself; these errors tend to be in his favor. But he doesn't dive off the deep end. He doesn't, for instance, undertake jobs until he's prepared to handle them to completion. This shows his awareness of his actual capabilities, but he never stops increasing them.

Finally, if I've given you an idea or two that'll help you in the creation of your own personal philosophy, then the purpose of this chapter has been served. When you ultimately decide you have built for yourself a philosophy by which you can guide your life, then perhaps you'll agree even more with Da Vinci that "The life that is well spent is a long life."

MILLIONAIRE SECRET#12

How to Release the Limitless Power of Your Psychic Wealth Machine -- the Amazing "Creative Generator" of Limitless Riches

If you'll trust your inner mind, you'll get more sound guidance and correct answers from it than you've ever imagined possible. It is, in effect, a computer capable of storing and providing feedback of a limitless amount of information, a psychic wealth machine that works night and day for you without your having to lift a finger.

But if you're like most persons, you have a tendency to distrust your inner mind. For instance, when a flash-thought passes through a man's mind as to what he should do about a problem confronting him, he dismisses it as a "hunch;" a woman calls the same process "intuition."

It's neither; what actually happens is that your inner mind attempts to feedback to you the solution to your problem. More often than not, though, you permit your conscious mind to interfere, to assume control, and negate the answer that comes out of your inner mind.

I'm using the term "inner mind" for what you may call the "subconscious mind." In actuality, the new science of "Cybernetics" has proven the so-called "subconscious mind" isn't a "mind" at all, but rather a mechanism—a goal-striving "servo-mechanism" composed of the brain and nervous system, which is used by and directed by the mind.

The latest, and most useful concept is that man doesn't have two "minds," that is, a conscious one and a subconscious one. Instead, he has a mind, or consciousness, which "operates" an automatic, goal-striving machine (an inner mind), which for want of a better definition I call the "Creative Generator" of Limitless Riches.

This Creative Generator within you is impersonal. It works automatically and impersonally to achieve goals of success and happiness, or failure and unhappiness, depending upon the goals you yourself set for it. Present it with "success-oriented" goals and it functions as a "success mechanism," present it with negative goals and it functions as a "failure mechanism."

William James, an American philosopher, said the power to move the world is in your Creative Generator. Your Creative Generator is one of infinite intelligence and boundless wisdom. Whatever you impress upon it, your Creative Generator will do everything it can to bring it about. So, you therefore must impress your Creative Generator with the right ideas and constructive thoughts.

You accept, I'm sure, the fundamental principle that progess is mental in origin; that what you plan to do must first have the approval of your mind. Therefore, you'll agree further that only self-influenced people lead the most successful lives. They are all people with high standards of their importance to themselves. This self-influence comes through the use of their Creative Generator.

If you, for instance, think negatively, destructively, and viciously, these thoughts, which are self-influenced, generate destructive emotions which must be expressed and find an outlet. On the other hand, if you think positively, constructively, your Creative Generator will also see that they're expressed in a constructive way.

Let's digress, briefly, and consider the make-up of the human brain, a mechanism so incredible and so fantastic that it's difficult for the limited mind of man to comprehend, to grasp the meaning of it.

Carefully shielded by a bony skull, the human brain weighs about three pounds and occupies about 90 cubic inches of space. It is a marvel of complexity and miniaturization. For within your brain are about 10 billion nerve cells called neurons and about 100 billion other cells called glia—110 billion functioning components packed into the size of a human head. It transmits its messages through an electrochemical system.

Your brain's constant electrochemical activity not only informs you of the external universe that surrounds you, but it also monitors and regulates and internal environment within you. Your brain receives information as electrical signals pouring in from the eyes, ears, nose, tongue, and fingers, and its neurons can simultaneously process and interpret these signals; and it stores the information for later recall.

Since you are equipped with this marvelous biological mechanism, you have the innate ability to achieve any goal you set for yourself—you have only to learn to use your brain to a fuller capacity. Thus, it is a psychic wealth machine that can bring you anything you want—quickly, easily, and practically without effort.

You know, then, that your Creative Generator accepts what is impressed upon it and what you consciously believe; it's amenable to suggestion. And such suggestion can be either autosuggestion (suggesting something definite and specific to yourself) or heterosuggestion (suggestions from another person).

You can, for instance, use autosuggestion to banish your fears and other negative conditions that confront you.

Let's use an example: Suppose you're having difficulty with your marriage. You can use your Creative Generator through autosuggestion to help you improve the relationship between you and your wife. Simply say to yourself each night prior to sleep for one month: "From now on I'm going to attempt to better understand my wife's viewpoint. I'm going to create ways that will help us have a better marriage. Every day I'm becoming more thoughtful, more considerate, and more understanding. My new attitude will infect my wife with a happier disposition. This new attitude of mine is now becoming my normal, natural state of mind."

But remember that when you are seeking an answer to a problem, your Creative Generator will respond, but it expects you to come to a decision and a true judgment in your conscious mind.

How often, for instance, do answers to your problems come when you're in the twilight zone, when your brain is relaxed, just before sleep comes? They come from your Creative Generator, which never sleeps.

The power of your Creative Generator is beyond comprehension. It inspires you, and it discloses to you names, facts, and scenes from your storehouse of memory. In addition, it controls your heartbeat, your blood circulation, and regulates your digestion, assimilation, and elimination. It is a mighty Invisible Servant with limitless power.

Your thought, as you go to sleep, arouses the powerful latency that is within you. In seeking the solution to your problems, as you approach sleep, you simply think quietly about right action which means that you are using the infinite intelligence of your Creative Generator to the point where it begins to use you. From there on, your course of action is directed and controlled by the subjective wisdom within your Creative Generator. Your decision, then, will be the correct one.

Believe it when I tell you that your Creative Generator controls all the functions and processes of your body and it knows the answers to all your problems. For it to bring you an automatic income for life is child's play to the mighty powers involved.

If you could, for instance, totally recall everything that is stored in your Creative Generator, you'd be the mental wizard of our age. But we haven't yet learned to do that; so far in our development we've learned only to recall a small fraction of the information stored within our brain.

There is, however, a method by which you can trigger the storehouse of information in your Creative Generator. Let's explore the method:

You know, for instance, that the part of the creative process that calls for little or no conscious effort is known as incubation. Incubation, as I use it here, simply means the phenomenon by which ideas spontaneously well up into your consciousness.

Incubation often results in "bright" ideas, and because the flashes are sometimes sudden, it's been referred to as "the period of luminous surprise." William Shakespeare called incubation "the spell in which imagination bodies forth the forms of things unknown." Writers know the value of incubation. They let their ideas simmer for a time before they put them on paper.

But, remember, your Creative Generator must be presented with a problem before it can solve it. In other words, I'm not discussing day dreaming, or wishful thinking. I'm suggesting you present your Creative Generator with a "success-oriented" problem and then let it help you solve it.

I've found that on many occasions I've given my own Creative Generator a problem to solve just before I fell to sleep; when I awoke the correct answer was in my conscious mind. There are other ways to trigger your Creative Generator. Lowell Thomas, the broadcaster and world traveler, uses a "deliberate, sustained period of silence—just an hour of silence, sitting still, neither reading nor looking upon anything in particular." A simple way to court illumination and solution to your problem is to take a walk.

One caution; when an idea comes to you on how to solve the problem you face, write it down. If you don't it may flee from your conscious mind and never return. I use a self-memo pad by my bed to jot down ideas I have that I want to recall in the morning. I also carry a notebook in my pocket so that whenever an idea occurs to me, no matter where I am, I write it down.

You must, however, present your Creative Generator with a clear-cut goal, objective, or problem for it to work on. Your self-image prescribes the limits of the accomplishment of any particular goals. It prescribes the "area of the possible."

Your Creative Generator, then, works upon information and data fed into it (facts, thoughts, beliefs, interpretations). Through your attitudes and interpretations of situations, you "describe" to your Creative Generator the problem to be worked upon.

How do you "describe" the problem to be worked upon by your Creative Generator? I suggest this method:

Write down on a piece of paper the problem confronting you to which you need a solution. Under it list all the facets to the problem that must be considered. Now set the paper aside, lie back in your chair, and relax. Under these conditions your Creative Generator can more easily function. Let your mind wander wherever it likes, don't attempt to focus it, give it all the leeway it needs. Before long it will begin to bring into sharp focus the problem you've presented it. Ultimately you'll get the solution you seek.

A quiet, peaceful, relaxed attitude of the mind prevents extraneous matter and false ideas from interfering with your mental absorption of your problem. Furthermore, in a quiet, passive, and receptive attitude of mind, effort is reduced to a minimum.

When you use this technique, you're, in effect, self-influencing yourself. You're influencing your Creative Generator, which, whether or not you acknowledge it, exerts a continuous influence over your life; a dominating influence that is in force 24 hours a day. When you lack control over it, it takes you on an unpredictable, "take-a-chance" course in life. When you control it, it'll guide you unerringly along a predetermined course, a course of your own choosing.

There are two kinds of influences shaping your life. As I mentioned earlier, one is "outside" (heterosuggestion), which often seems to stand like a monster over you. "Outside" influence always seems to be exerting pressure on your will, forcing you to do things, or to cause things to happen to you, simply because such influences seem too big for you to resist.

The second is "inner" (autosuggestion) influence, that of the power of your Creative Generator. This is the dynamic power that's never turned off. But if you don't use this power, or don't know how, you may be inclined to say it can "go along" with "outside" influence. At such times, if your Creative Generator could speak, it'd say, "My master wants to act that way, he wants to be directed by 'outside' influences, so I'll support his desire."

Your Creative Generator, however, under your control, can do remarkable things; its power can become useful and productive in your life. As I've repeatedly emphasized, you can choose your own kind of life, but to do so you must bridle your Creative Generator—you must make it work for you.

Put still another way, you must make your Creative Generator your active, and productive partner. Every person who's achieved success, every person of importance has formed a working alliance with this partner.

You may, at this point, say: "All this about a Creative Generator is simply a bunch of mumbo-jumbo; it's a nebulous, intangible theory that no one has ever been able to reduce to a practical, workable technique."

If you believe that, let's see if there is any basis for your belief.

Do you, for instance, drive a car "automatically?" Certainly you don't. You drive by reason of habit, and the habit is the result of prompting your Creative Generator to get you to repeat an action that matches a pattern previously filed away; subconsciously. You have scores of such habits stored away in your Creative Generator. They govern most of what you do.

They make life easier, or harder. They serve or defeat your purpose of life. Habit formation and control are major functions of your inner mind, your Creative Generator.

You know, as do I, that we as humans are creatures of habit. You learned to swim, drive a car, ride a bicycle, dance, and roller skate by consciously doing these things over and over again until they established tracks in your Creative Generator—until they become the automatic habit action of your Creative Generator.

You may call this process "second nature," but in reality, you've fed the habit pattern into your brain and your brain feeds it back when you call upon it to do so.

If this is true, and I believe it is, then it follows that you are free to choose a good habit or a bad habit. If you repeat a negative thought or act over a period of time, you'll be under the compulsion of a habit. The law of your Creative Generator is compulsion.

But still another function of your Creative Generator is to evaluate experience. It classifies them as positive or negative.

Thirdly, your Creative Generator also records and decides the disposition of attitudes.

Let there be no misunderstanding, however; knowledge (education) is the best source of your inner power; it'll enable you to use your Creative Generator at its greatest capacity. The more information you store in your human computer, the more you'll be able to recall to use when you have need of it.

The point, then, is this: You have within you a built-in guidance system or goal-striving device, put there by nature to help you achieve your goal. So, begin now to harness your Creative Generator—use it as a principal weapon in your success arsenal through positive, self-influenced action.

MILLIONAIRE SECRET#13

How to Achieve --and Keep -- Huge Personal Wealth Despite the Current U.S. Tax Structure

G. Ralph Bartolme of Arcadia, California, a suburb of Los Angeles, is a self-made millionaire who knows that a man creates his own opportunities to achieve huge personal wealth. Today, Bartolme lives with his wife of 25 years, Barbara, and four children in an upper-middle-class neighborhood; he owns three dogs, a ping pong table, and an average size swimming pool is situated in the north end of his acre of property. Every morning at 8:30 a.m., Bartolme drives his Cadillac to the corporate offices of the VSI Corporation, a large publicly owned metals firm in Pasadena located just a few minutes from his home.

It wasn't always that way for Ralph Bartolme—he began life in near abject poverty. His achievements have come from his own efforts.

What distinguishes Bartolme from the ranks of the middle class is that he's one of the expanding number of corporate millionaires, men who're using the techniques of stock options to amass wealth. He's estimated to be worth a personal fortune of $2 million.

It's no accident that Bartolme became wealthy. He, like all other successful men, based his climb to success on an all-powerful desire to achieve a specific goal, sound preparation, and a willingness to take whatever risks necessary to reach his objective. And he learned early as a boy that a man, for the most part, makes his own opportunities.

The story of how Ralph Bartolme became wealthy has almost become a classic in American business history. It's the saga of a boy born into a depressed neighborhood of poor immigrants in a large city who literally fought his way out and up with an awesome degree of determination and will to win.

Along the way to becoming a winner, Bartolme made his own opportunities.

He was born in the Polish-Italian neighborhood of Austin, a westside Chicago suburb, in 1918. His father, a tailor, and his mother, who helped, were Italian immigrants. Enough money on which to live was always a challenge to the Bartolme family, which included three girls in addition to Ralph.

Bartolme decided early that he wouldn't join a street gang, the popular thing to do in the neighborhood at the time. He knew such an association would interfere with his all-powerful desire to make a success of himself. His attitude caused him to be looked upon as "strange" by his contemporaries. Nevertheless, he had decided he'd control his own destiny; not let others, including a street gang, do it for him.

Since money in his family was in short supply, Bartolme helped put himself through Austin High School by working in the cafeteria. He was, in fact, the only kid in his neighborhood who went beyond high school.

Bartolme said he'd decided early that he wouldn't succeed in the way he wanted to without a college education. So, while he continued to live at home, he attended Roosevelt University in Chicago and received a bachelor of science degree in commerce in 1939.

"I averaged working 20 hours a week during my entire four years of college in addition to a fulltime summer job in a delicatessen near home," he recalled. "I had one odd job as a light bulb washer that paid me 35 cents an hour."

Bartolme and a friend devised an ingenious scheme to add further to their incomes. They ran dart games, bean bag and other types of concessions for social functions sponsored by charitable institutions to raise money. The two college boys split the proceeds with the institutions.

These activities were just some of the opportunities Ralph Bartolme created for himself—he'd create many others on his path to wealth, prestige, and happiness.

After he graduated from college, he went to work for the Chicago Relief Administration. Six months later, he left to join the Illinois State Department of Unemployment Compensation where he remained until he was drafted into the U.S. Army in 1941.

During World War II Bartolme rose to the rank of Chief Warrant Officer in the U.S. Army Air Corps. He did so, again, by creating his own opportunity—he became an expert in personnel administration.

When he was released from the U.S. Army in January 1946 he obtained a job as a U.S. Internal Revenue Service agent.

Up until now Bartolme's career, his progress, hadn't been much different than any other 1939 college graduate who'd spent four years in the Army during a war. But there was a difference, even if it wasn't obvious. Bartolme had an all-powerful desire to achieve a specific goal and he was determined to reach it.

How he did it is best told by Bartolme himself. On a recent day in Pasadena he used forceful, persuasive tones, as he discussed in detail his philosophy of success and his own personal record of growth and achievement:

"My philosophy adds up to the attainment of happiness not only selfishly for the individual, but also for the people with whom one associates," Bartolme said.

"All of us have a different set of objectives in life and a different set of standards which result in the attainment of happiness. To some people, material rewards of the accumulation of material things in life is the only form of happiness they know and aspire to. Others find happiness in this world by preparing for the next world. To them material things have very minor significance."

Bartolme, then, as other successful men, believes a man must have aspirations—goals—before he can begin to succeed. Once they have been established, the next step is to do whatever is required to achieve them.

"First of all," he said, "each individual generally aspires to that which will give him his greatest happiness in this life whatever that may be. In my own particular instance, happiness started with the attainment of security in the forms of a strong educational background and the later accumulation of material things. This is only natural considering the financial difficulties of my early years. both the depressed economics in my home life and the difficulty in working my way through college.

"However, since security is attained according to the standard established by the individual, happiness then takes on a broader aspect which goes beyond the selfish instinct. This is concern for your fellow man which is reflected in part in the way you conduct yourself in relationships with the people around you personally and in business."

It's such a philosophy that has enabled Bartolme to achieve his own success. Today at 50 he's senior vice-president for finance and law and secretary-treasurer of the VSI Corporation which did nearly $80 million business in 1968. The company's aerospace fasteners are used in 90 percent of the commerical and military aircraft now being built in the Western world, it produces about 80 percent of the mold bases used by the plastic industry, and it produces short run metal stampings, magnetic tape recording heads and metal cosmetic containers.

Based on his background, experience and achievements, there are few men in the nation better qualified to reveal the formula for achieving huge personal wealth than Ralph Bartolme.

"For those who seek material things for personal satisfaction and happiness the solutions are quite simple," he said. "I can best describe them by relating my particular situation and growth experience.

"My life had a most humble beginning in a depressed area of Chicago where I was surrounded with illiterates and those who taught college and higher learning were for the privileged few. However, I was tempted early in life by opportunities to enjoy material things because I began working at a very young age. From this experience came very tangible goals. I can only say that the first ingredient to success must be firm dedication to the ideals and objectives you've established for yourself.

"Had there not been a very strong dedication and will to follow through to completion of my education, I'm certain I would have fallen by the wayside," Bartolme said.

So, briefly restated, Bartolme insists the first key to success, to the attainment of success, is the fixing of an all-powerful desire to achieve a specific goal. Then you must have the education, the staying power, to attain it. As he said, "You must carry through no matter what temptations might be presented to deter you."

Bartolme believes that for a person to achieve success he must have average intelligence and considerable common sense intelligence.

"Both are essential in evaluating opportunities from a practical and pecuniary standpoint," he said. "Not having the advantage of guidance in early years, my main objective was to cash in on opportunities on a day-to-day basis without consideration of long-term plans. This led me to accept a position with the Chicago Relief Administration upon graduation from college because that was the one job that would pay me the most money immediately. Later, working for the Internal Revenue Service introduced me to the ways of making money and was probably the greatest experience I have received as to how to do it."

Bartolme said the U.S. Internal Revenue Service taught him that the method to achieve—and keep—huge personal wealth, considering the current U.S. tax structure, was for a person to go into business for himself where capital gains are possible or work for a company and share in its prosperity through stock options. He said it was exceedingly difficult to accumulate any form of wealth in our modern society through most other means.

Bartolme, then, believes there are only two ways in which to amass great personal wealth: (1) Operating a business for yourself where capital gains are possible, or (2) Working for a company and sharing in its earning through stock options.

He said that after a year-and-a-half with the Internal Revenue Service he thought he'd learned all he could from it. "It became obvious that the Government can give you experience and security, but no wealth," he said.

Bartolme's next step up the ladder to wealth came from his association with the General Electric Company, which he joined in 1948.

"General Electric Company, my next employer, provided me with an immediate advancement in income plus the opportunity to go to Law School on company time," he said. "After spending 10 years at General Electric in many facets of management including labor relations, tax management, manufacturing administration, coordination of management projects and a host of other general management programs, I decided that I still wasn't on the right road to a major material accumulation. General Electric couldn't provide the two necessary ingredients, i.e., a major stock option and a position in a company on the threshold of major expansion.

"Consequently, I realized that my accounting, legal and general management experience would be more valuable to a small company than to General Electric with its host of experience in all fields."

Bartolme decided to take a gigantic risk—an important element of achieving success. Although he's been assistant to the president and general manager to General Electric's X-Ray Corporation, and had obvious prospects for future advancement in the company, he believed greater opportunity lay elsewhere. So he resigned.

"I left General Electric for my present employer whose future at the time was questionable," Bartolme said. "However, the opportunity of amassing wealth was outstanding. Although my major objective and aim in life earlier was to find security, I was willing at this time to take the risk of leaving my secure position at General Electric because I felt that my academic background and experience had now equipped me to build my own security."

By his move, Bartolme, in effect, had again made his own opportunity.

"VSI Corporation has grown in a major way during my 12 years of association with the company and the stock has gone from the equivalent of $1.50 a share when I started to a current value of approximately $40 a share," he said. "My option has paid off and my objective was attained from a standpoint of financial means."

That, then, is Bartolme's success story. Could it be repeated today by a young man who also has the goal of achieving great wealth? Bartolme believes it can.

"My son tells me things are different today," Bartolme said. "Schools are more difficult and competition more keen. He says my success would be extremely difficult to match today. I can't accept this theory since I doubt that many young men could have had things more difficult than me in climbing the ladder.

"Given an above average common sense intelligence, some ingenuity, a little luck, the opportunity to go to school and above all the will power and dedication to accomplish an objective, there's no reason why a man can't achieve what I have."

What characteristics, then, does a young man need to duplicate a success story like Bartolme's?

"The characteristics he must have," said Ralph Bartolme, "are the industry to work way beyond what the average requirements are for young men and the willingness to set aside present pleasures in social life for the long range objectives of life.

"We see all too many young men today who are interested merely in obtaining all the comforts of life in the form of material things almost immediately," he said. "They don't wish to commit themselves to a long range objective because today's comfort is more important than tomorrow's prosperity and security. As a result they frequently go deeply into debt before they've found a foundation to grow from. Sacrifices must be made, effort must be above normal and dedication and will power must be at a high degree if the person with no financial endowment is to rise and succeed. For those willing to accept these sacrifices, the opportunities are as much available today, if not more so, than they were during my generation."

Bartolme's career, then, proves that the first jobs you hold have a great bearing on your future—probably more than you realize. They can either limit the development of your career or spur it on to growth and early success.

Therefore, to duplicate his success, you need to do these three things whether you're looking ahead to your first job or wondering whether you're in the right spot now: (1) Become a part of a growth industry; that is, connect with a firm that is forging ahead in such fields as electronics, chemicals, plastics, nuclear energy, and the like: (2) Seek out an expanding company, one that is known as a pace-setter in its field; and (3) Check for progressive management, make certain the company you know has a management team known for its enlightened leadership, modern-thinking, and development of executive talent.

Then, once you've joined an expanding company in a growth industry, work by the job, not by the clock; ask intelligent questions of those above you so that you can learn as much as you can quickly about the business: and volunteer whenever possible for the odd assignment—particularly the one your associates shun.

These are the elements that have worked for Ralph Bartolme; they also will work for you. They are, in effect, all part of the formula for achieving personal wealth.

MILLIONAIRE SECRET #14

How to Discover and Use the Master Money Formula that Brings the Biggest Rewards

In this book's first chapter, I stated a basic premise: You can control your destiny. If you truly want success, it can be yours, but you must have an all-powerful desire to achieve a specific goal, a willingness to act and take the needed risks, and you must apply yourself with every ounce of ability you possess. You must believe that, despite all obstacles, you can control your destiny if you focus your mind on worthwhile objectives.

Certainly, there are those who get off to a better start than others because of environment—family connections, wealth, educational background—and other factors, but it's the finish line that counts—that's where the measure of a man is taken.

And so, each suggestion in this book has had one purpose—to show you how to grasp and exercise control over your own destiny. Every success story in these pages has been recounted for one reason—to prove to you that others, no matter what their age or education, have exercised control over their fate and have been rewarded with success.

Now, as you enter the final pages, I'll show you, with examples, the master money formula that brings the biggest rewards. Its elements are present in every success story. Actually, this formula is a present summation of the main points of this book. The formula, in substance is this: The degree of your all-powerful desire to reach a specific goal, plus your willingness to act and take the necessary risks, multiplied by the intensity of your personal drive. These then, to repeat, are the major elements of the master money formula:

1. An all-powerful desire to achieve a specific goal.
2. Preparation to achieve your goal (education and experience).
3. Willingness to take necessary risks to achieve your goal.
4. Intensity of your personal drive.

You'll note that I don't include "breaks" or "luck" in the formula; I believe the success-oriented person makes his own "breaks" or "luck." Only the daydreamer, the wishful-thinker, counts on chance to help him achieve success—this book isn't for him.

I'm sure you've known failures who justified their lack of success on the basis of "the breaks have never come my way; I'm just unlucky." They have settled for doubt, discouragement, and the negative point of view. They've never learned the winner's philosophy of positive thinking and planning directed toward a positive goal backed up by enthusiasm, persistency, and a deep seated belief in himself.

So, let's now review the four elements in the framework of the master money formula:

First, an all-powerful desire to achieve a specific goal: you must decide what you want out of life, what you want to achieve, and you must want it so badly that you'll make any and every effort to attain your goal.

Let's for an example, look at one man who set money as his goal. He's Bart Lytton, the flamboyant financier, forced by creditors to relinquish control of the giant Lytton Financial Corporation in Los Angeles. Despite this, he has a seven-year contract with his savings and loan successors. It pays him $50,000 a year as a consultant, but it bars him from entering a competitive field.

Has this temporary setback discouraged Lytton from making an attempt to rebuild his fortune? Certainly not. Money is still his major goal and he says he plans to amass even more of it through the advertising business.

"The reason I've chosen advertising per se, say over public relations, is that there is now a small history of advertising agencies going public. And it's possible thereby to build a fortune," Lytton said. "Today you can't make and keep money making money—that is, by income, you have to make it in capital gains. In public relations I might earn a million dollars a year, but I'd be fortunate to keep a few hundred thousand of that. But if I build an advertising agency that made a million dollars it would have a market value of $15-20 million."

Lytton, a man who's never had his self-image or self-confidence questioned, believes he has the track record to do this. "In 10 years I built a little nothing company with capitalization of $125,000 to one with assets of $600 million," he said.

Lytton, at 55, doesn't fear the future nor does he worry about having practically to make a new start at an age when many other men start contemplating retirement.

"I don't have to belabor it, but I do have a unique track record in business promotion, and advertising is a signal part of that," he said. "And I have entree—I can open doors and see chief executives throughout the country certainly as easily as the biggest people in the advertising field."

When Lytton enters the advertising field, he'll, in effect, be starting his third major career. Before he became a financier he was a screenwriter.

What can Lytton offer the advertising business that it doesn't already have—something that'll enable him to amass another fortune?

"The advertising business today," he said, "is clearly a growth industry, but it's suffering from a plethora of unwitting mediocrity. Most agencies are intimidated by fear of losing an account should they resort to originality.

"There are some good ones, but the average is pedestrian like the average anything else. And it's pedestrian in an economy that's no longer pedestrian. The race will go ultimately to the swift. There will be fewer and bigger agencies."

So what Bart Lytton proposes to bring to the advertising business is greater originality—few who know him doubt that he'll pull it off; for he's never lost sight of his major goal—money.

I have quoted Lytton at some length on his philosophy of how to make money and how to operate an advertising agency so that you'll get an idea of how a successful man thinks; how even when fortunes turn against him he doesn't give up, but rather looks to meet new challenges, new opportunities.

Now for the second element of the master money formula: Preparation to achieve your goal. This includes formal education, night school and correspondence courses, and independent study through a self-improvement reading program. It is such a background that is a major component of your success.

In some professions, like medicine, law, engineering, or teaching, a formal college education is a prerequisite. In other fields, men with little scholastic training have achieved outstanding success. But remember: What these self-made men lacked in formal education, they made up in self-improvement programs designed to fill their education void.

One such man is Robert F. Six, president of Continental Airlines, who was a high school dropout. He educated himself through self-study and on-the-job training. Six started his aviation career as a barnstorming pilot who raced airplanes around California. As its co-founder Six was Continental Airlines head pilot when it started 30 years ago. He built it from two airplanes into a commerical airline that in 1968 had operating revenues of about $190 million.

So with Robert F. Six it has been self-education plus experience that has enabled him to build a giant commercial airline and in the process make himself wealthy.

The third element of the master money formula is: The willingness to take necessary risks to achieve your goal. You must, as has been repeatedly emphasized in this book, be willing to bet on yourself and take a calculated chance.

Stanley L. Ross, president of California Investors, a Los Angeles investment company, bet on himself and within 15 years he was worth a personal fortune of $2 million and was earning an annual salary of $72,000.

His start was typical of many another young American of his time. In June 1942 he earned an Associate of Arts degree from the University of California at Los Angeles. Then from mid-1942 until early 1946 he served in the U.S. Army during World War II. For two years after he was discharged he was a salesman of paper products. In 1948 he became an account executive for a West Coast advertising agency. By 1950 his business career was moving along nicely, but not as rapidly as Ross would have liked.

"A friend of mine was doing quite well in the mutual funds business," Ross said. "He convinced me of both the merits of mutual fund investing and the need to bring 'Wall Street to Main Street.' "

Ross tossed over his ad agency job and began to sell mutual

funds; later he established his own investment company, California Investors.

"The first year California Investors was in business gross sales approximated $4.5 million," Ross said. "Gross sales amounted to $42 million in 1967 and our 1968 gross was about $53 million."

Ross was willing to take a risk; he threw up a secure job for the uncertainty of going out on his own. But he had the self-confidence, the good self-image, and the self-discipline, to independently make it on his own.

What, then, in Ross's judgment, should a man do if he wants to enter the investment business and make a success of it?

"First, a man must thoroughly understand and be committed to the principles under which our capitalistic society functions," he said. "Second, he must learn every pertinent aspect of the investment securities business and develop the ability to communicate accurately and candidly with the public. Third, he must be willing to work hard in the development of his clientele, exercise considerable self-discipline and sincerely want to be of service."

Ross, like other successful men, is goal-oriented. He said it's important, for instance, for a securities salesman to always have a goal in front of him.

"So far as the amount of his sales per year," Ross said, "it gets back to the importance of a sales goal and in this area I think it critical that anyone in our business closely adheres to an annual goal which is broken down to the amount of sales required each business day of the week. Only in this way does the goal become meaningful and it is possible to achieve it. Equally important, each year's goal should be more than the representative feels he can really achieve. However, by steadily employing the 'think big' philosophy, he'll probably do a great deal more than he would have otherwise."

Each of the three men that have so far been used as examples of unusual success have also had tremendous intensity in their personal drive, the fourth element in the master success formula.

So has Ann-Margret, the young movie actress who today earns $500,000 a year. The leggy, red-haired beauty never doubted that she'd reach stardom. "I'm very determined," she says, exuding self-confidence and ambition. "I decided when I was four that I was going to be an entertainer, and I've been taking singing and dancing lessons ever since."

What has given her such intensity of personal drive? She insists it isn't money, even though she makes more in one year than the average college graduate makes in a lifetime of earnings.

Ann-Margret, who was born Ann-Margret Olsson in Sweden in 1941, came with her parents to the United States in 1946. During her grade school and high school years in Wilmette, Illinois, her life was an endless succession of singing and dancing performances.

In her freshman year at Northwestern University she and three boys formed a jazz combo. They began a series of summer nightclub appearances. She decided not to return to college. Later a Las Vegas appearance was the turning point in her career—it got her a recording contract. From that she moved on and upward into the movies.

Today the top performers in the entertainment world who know her generally agree Ann-Margret's success is due more to her intensity than her talent. As one of her managers has said, "She wouldn't flip you 'cause she sings so good, dances so good or has such a great figure—but, oh, that desire!"

A Hollywood director has said of her, "I've been in this business 30 years and seen no one with her fire. When she goes, it's electric."

Ann-Margret herself admits she's resolute. "I won't step on anybody," she says, "but I won't let anyone interfere with my being a performer. It's all work and planning. No one ever forced me to rehearse and rehearse. I thought it was a privilege to work as hard as I have, and I still think so."

So, Ann-Margret combined all four elements of the master money formula, as you must. She had an all-powerful desire to achieve a specific goal, she prepared herself to achieve it, she was willing to take whatever risks were necessary, and she had a relentless personal drive.

If one person can achieve such success, so can another; but let me point out that success is a personal thing. What may be success to Ann-Margret may not be success to you and vice versa.

You yourself must set your standards of success. How high do you want to shoot? You may decide to enter politics. What will satisfy you? The job of mayor or governor? You may decide on business. Which do you choose? Head of a local department store or president of a national corporation? This you'll have to decide.

No matter what your goal, though, your greatest satisfaction will not be the reward. It'll be the exhilaration of achievement. It's the race that's the fun. And the sooner you get started, the quicker you'll find the excitement and challenge that each new day holds for you.

MILLIONAIRE SECRET#15

How to Set Up a Magic System that Points the Way to Wealth-Building Opportunities Automatically Year after Year

Do you have a built-in key to personal and financial success?

Can nearly anyone, regardless of his monetary worth or station in life, achieve the kind of success that brings him money, influence, and happiness?

Is there a magic system you can set up that will point the way to wealth-building opportunities for you automatically, year after year?

My research indicates "Yes" is the answer to all three questions.

"Success is a state of mind," William Lawson, Chief of Public Information of the California State Department of Human Resources Development once told me, "and once the state is acquired a man's achievements can be limitless."

Bill Lawson should know. He emigrated to the United States from Borneo in 1959 with a small amount of savings in the bank. Within 10 years after his arrival in the U.S., he'd established a successful public relations and advertising firm and had achieved a high position in California's State Government.

Bill Lawson knew what he wanted. He established his goals, he had an overpowering desire to achieve them, and he set about reaching them without regard to luck—he made his own luck.

"Shallow men believe in luck," said Ralph Waldo Emerson. There isn't any luck, as Bill Lawson knows, along the path a man follows to personal and financial success. What are along that path to success are hours of study, well-conceived and executed plans, specific goals, and lots of hard work.

Why do we all want to achieve success?

Let's admit it—we all crave attention. We want to be important, immortal. We want to do things that will make people exclaim, "Isn't he wonderful?"

The best and most constructive way for you and I to gain the attention we crave, to acquire our piece of immortality, is to achieve success.

Let's take, for instance, the circumstances of James Joseph Ling, whose success story I told in Chapter 2. Today Jim Ling is one of America's richest men. But in early 1946 he was just out of the U.S. Navy, had no occupational skill, and little money.

Ling decided the way he'd begin his climb to success would be to become a licensed electrical engineer. So he read and memorized two books: *The Electrical Engineers Handbook* and *The National Electrical Code.* On his second try he passed the city of Dallas electrical engineering examination. He was 22 at the time.

But Jim Ling didn't want to be an electrical engineer working for someone else—he wanted to be an electrical contractor running his own business.

So, with $3,000 that he'd saved from his Navy pay in World War II, Ling opened his own contracting business. That was his beginning; within 20 years he'd become a multi-millionaire.

What, then, were the elements of Ling's success?

First, it was, as he admits, the desire to succeed, and succeed rapidly.

Second, his staying power, "It's the staying power that makes the difference between winners and losers," he said.

The point I made in Chapter 2, using Jim Ling as an example, is that nothing can stymie a man with the desire, the determination, to succeed.

But, at this point, you're saying to yourself, "How can I relate my circumstances to these wealthy men and women I've read about in this book? Here I am a guy with practically nothing in the bank and I owe money on my house and car."

Well, those were the circumstances of the men and women in this book when they began their climb to success. That's why I chose their stories to tell in making points, and laying out a blueprint, that, you too, can use for your own financial advancement. What they have done, you can do.

Ken Riley, for instance, whose story I told in Chapter 3, said there were four major elements that enabled him to become a millionaire. They are, he said:

"1. A burning desire and driving ambition to be wealthy.

"2. A tolerant and understanding wife, Melinda, without whom I couldn't have succeeded so rapidly.

"3. A book, *Law of Success* by Napoleon Hill, and

"4. An inspirational record, 'Strangest Secret' by Earl Nightingale distributed by Success Motivation Institute, Inc., Waco, Texas,"

But where you ask, did Ken Riley get the money to start his climb to financial success?

Simply put, he earned it and saved it until he had enough to make a down payment on his first piece of real estate property. Riley worked in the stock room of a retail store, he worked on construction projects, and he took jobs wherever he could find them to earn extra money.

Then, when he'd saved enough, he used his savings for the down payment on the first house he constructed. When it was finished he sold it at a profit. He used a profit from that sale to make the down payment on a larger property. This was the way he entered the general contracting business—he kept pyramiding his investments.

Ken Riley's fortune formula worked for him—he insists it'll work for anyone who'll adopt it.

Honolulu's William Koon Kee Mau, whose success story I recount in Chapter 5, followed a path similar to Riley's in his rise to great wealth.

Bill Mau started his career as an elevator operator, then he worked in an advertising agency, and finally obtained a U.S. Civil Service job. But these were only progressive steps in his climb to wealth. All the while he worked at these jobs he saved as much of his salary as he could, and he was always on the lookout for opportunities. His first independent investment was a hamburger stand that he started with money he'd saved plus money he was able to borrow from friends. At first he kept his civil service job and worked at it by day while he manned his hamburger stand at night.

But the essential point about Bill Mau's career is that he always knew what he wanted and he refused to permit anything to interfere with the achievement of his objectives.

And neither Bill Mau nor any of the other men and women whose success stories I've told in this book ever permitted themselves to entertain the possibility of failure.

Let's as an example, look again at the career of Patrick Henry, American patriot, who failed repeatedly, but never accepted failure. There is a difference between failing at something you attempt and being a failure. The difference is that the failure, once he's failed, never again attempts to succeed. This wasn't Patrick Henry's way.

By the time he was 23, Patrick Henry had failed twice as a storekeeper and once a farmer. But he refused to quit.

"What can I do to make myself a success?" he asked. The answer: become a lawyer; but how, without time or money, could he study law? He had a wife, four children, and burdensome debts.

Nevertheless, Patrick Henry borrowed a set of law books and studied them relentlessly. Then he traveled to Williamsburg, the colonial capital of Virginia, and presented himself for examination. He passed and was admitted to the Virginia Bar.

The remainder of Patrick Henry's career is history—he went from success to greater success the rest of his life. And what success he achieved; the man who refused to accept failure.

So, the important question for you, as one who wants to make a success of himself, is whether you really want to succeed. If your answer is "Yes," then you also need to answer these questions with honesty:

How strong is my desire to succeed?

Do I have enough personal drive to succeed?

Can I discipline myself constantly to assure myself that I'm doing everything that I must do to achieve my goal?

Will I do what's necessary—in time, study, working—to achieve my goal?

If you can answer "Yes" to these, and you mean it, then you have the ingredients of a successful man or woman. But let me re-emphasize an additional ingredient that you must have to succeed—staying power. You must be able to accept setbacks without giving up; you mustn't let temporary failures force you to give up; and, no matter what, you must keep your eye on and direct all your efforts toward the goal you've set for yourself.

These are the qualities that separate the successful man and women from the failures. You must either have them or develop them.

Ed Robinson, of Oceanside, California, whose story I tell in Chapter 7, developed these qualities quickly and used them to amass wealth for himself in a rather small city.

When Ed Robinson began his climb to success he was in his mid-40's, he had a mortgaged home, an automobile he was making monthly payments on, and two children he was helping put through college.

On top of these drawbacks, Ed Robinson reacted counter to the millions of men and women who each year leave small cities for metropolitan ones because they believe their hometowns offer them scant opportunity.

Nevertheless, Robinson's success story proves, at least in his instance, that they could find success at home if they had the desire, ambition, and personal drive to go after it.

How did Ed Robinson achieve his success? How did he set up magic system to find the wealth-building opportunities he needed?

He simply applied for a job as an insurance salesman, got it, and set about becoming the most successful insurance man in his city. And he did this by establishing goals for himself and then setting out, regardless of obstacles, to achieve them.

The method used by Robinson didn't require money to get him started on his success ladder. However, the goal you have in mind may take capital. Where do you get it?

In seeking capital to start your own business career, the first thing to do is to establish personal contact with your own banker. The next time you go into your bank to deposit a check or draw out money, look up the manager. Introduce yourself to him. Let him know who you are, what you do, and when you have a chance discuss your business and financial goals with him.

Such a contact is vital to you if you intend to go into business for yourself and use borrowed money to get started. If your banker personally knows you, you'll stand a better chance of getting your initial loan.

Unless you already have property to use as collateral that you can pledge to guarantee the repayment of a loan, you'll want a personal loan to get started. In general, to qualify for a personal loan of $1,000 to $5,000 you must meet these qualifications:

1. Own your business or have a steady job.

2.Prove that you've worked for one organization for six months or more.

3. Establish that you've lived at the same address for six months or more.

4. Own an automobile or other personal property or have a telephone in your home.

But if you need money to start your climb to success, don't limit yourself as to where you look for it.

For instance, check the Yellow Pages in you telephone book. You'll find that most banks and finance companies that make personal loans will have display ads in it. Phone them and ask them to send you information on how they make personal loans.

There are still other sources for money you may want to pursue. These include:

1. Personal friends. You may find one or more of your friends who'll be interested in investing in the enterprise you're developing.

2. Religious organizations that may have money available for investment.

3. Business firms, financial brokers, real estate firms, insurance companies, and financial advisors often have money for investment purposes.

In addition, the Government Printing Office, Washington, D.C., 20402, issues valuable publications on business financing and operations. They are: *A Handbook of Small Business Finance,* 50 cents; and *A Survey of Federal Government Publications of Interest to Small Business,* also 50 cents.

If you've tried every possibility I've mentioned so far and you still haven't been successful in getting the financing you need, don't give up. There's still one more where you're likely to hit a home run. It's the Small Business Administration (SBA), Washington, D.C.

The Small Business Administration loans money to individuals so they can go into business for themselves or expand businesses they already own. And if you're already a small businessman, you may be surprised to learn that it also offers you valuable non-loan assistance on management, marketing, financing, and so on.

But let me emphasize here: Borrowed money is of little use to you unless you put it to work earning money for yourself. So, you must be alert for wealth opportunities around you or that come your way.

How, you ask, do I find wealth-building opportunities? These are some of the ways:

1. Look for possibilities in the Business Opportunities columns in the classified ad section of your daily newspapers. And don't overlook your regional and neighborhood weekly newspapers. They, too, often contain opportunities that may appeal to you.

2. Talk to businessmen. Ask their advice. Ask them to suggest opportunities they may know of but can't take advantage of themselves.

3. Read widely. Become a regular patron of your public library. Get to know the librarian and ask her to keep an eye out for the new books on business and finance that may interest you.

4. Read business publications. *The Wall Street Journal, Business Week, Nation's Business, Barron's Fortune, Success Unlimited,* and so on. If you can't afford to subscribe to them, go to your library regularly and read them. You'll find in them an endless number of wealth-building opportunities.

And above all, make use of your friends—particularly those in business and who understand financing, business management, and how to locate and develop wealth-building opportunities.

If you believe you need to increase your knowledge of business and finance enroll in college and university night courses in your area. Take courses in business administration, accounting, marketing, salesmanship, real estate, banking, investments and so on.

On the other hand, if you can't attend resident courses on a regular basis, enroll in correspondence schools. I recommend these three:

LaSalle Extension University, 417 South Dearborn Street, Chicago, Illinois 60605

Alexander Hamilton Institute, 235 East 42nd Street, New York, New York 10017

International Correspondence Schools, Scranton, Pennsylvania 18515

All three of these schools will permit you to pay for your courses on the monthly installment plan. Write them a letter, tell them what your goal is, and they'll provide you with information on what courses you should take in your efforts to achieve it.

If you've read this far, you know every millionaire mentioned in this book did two essential things to achieve his wealth:

1. He made up his mind, developed an overwhelming desire to achieve wealth because he knew the comfortable, satisfying status of wealth was precisely what he wanted.

2. He wanted wealth so earnestly that he was willing to do something everyday of his life to help himself achieve his goal.

These essentials apply equally to women.

Let's briefly return to Linda Sinay who operates her own advertising agency in Los Angeles. In five years she developed her agency from an at-home operation with no capital to a current annual billing of more than $1 million a year. I told her success story in Chapter 9.

But what is Linda Sinay's success formula? In her own words, it's this:

I learned early I couldn't work for anybody. I had to do it myself.
I still do. And I try to hire people just like that. There's no mystique.
I'm not a witch. But I know if you have confidence, know who you
are and work hard, you can make it. It's there to be had.

It's there for you, too.

Laurie Hancock (Chapter 10) also knew it was there, and she
began to reach for it as a high school student in Thief River Falls,
Minnesota.

If there was one day in her life that can be pinpointed as the
precise day Laurie Hancock began her climb to wealth it was the
day she was selected the outstanding business student in her high
school and appointed after-school secretary to her principal.

Mrs. Hancock couldn't afford to go to college, but she had a
natural aptitude for business and an unrelenting desire to
achieve success.

Upon graduation from high school, Mrs. Hancock applied to
the president of the Union State Bank in Thief River Falls for
the job as the bank president's secretary. Her high school
principal, for whom she's been a part-time secretary, gave her
high recommendations for the job. She got it.

In her job with the bank, Laurie Hancock quickly learned
about banking, how businesses were financed, what businessmen needed to do to obtain loans for the expansion of the
businesses or to start new ones.

"I learned a great deal from my boss because I saw problems
and situations through his eyes and the psychology with which
he dealt with them," she said. "I learned so much, in fact, it was
an 'on-the-job' college education."

But being a secretary was only a beginning for Laurie
Hancock.

Later when she became involved in business on her own, she
applied ·the age-old principle "to be a success, discover a need
and fill it."

Laurie Hancock understood this to mean, as have other
successful men and women, that if you find people want

something they don't have, then you can become rich by providing them with it. Men and women have made themselves multimillionaires following this principle—frozen foods, canned baby food, wash-and-wear clothing—the list is endless.

In Laurie Hancock's case it was manufacturing better and more attractive outdoor redwood furniture.

She challenged her mind with these two questions as she designed and manufactured better furniture: "Is what I have in mind better, stronger, lovelier, more practical and useful? Does it provide a chance for greater returns, or insure an easier way of life?"

When she got the answer "Yes" to both questions, then she knew she was on the right path.

Laurie Hancock had an all-powerful desire to achieve a specific goal. She achieved it and today enjoys the comforts that wealth can bring.

Still another person who had that all-power desire to achieve a specific goal is G. Ralph Bartolme, whose success story I told in Chapter 13. In his advice to those who want to duplicate his success he said, "You must carry through no matter what temptations might be presented to deter you."

Bartolme began his climb to success by getting a job with the U.S. Internal Revenue Service. On that job he learned that one method that could be used to achieve great personal wealth, despite the U.S. tax structure, was for a person to go into business for himself where capital gains are possible or work for a company and share in its prosperity through stock options.

"After a year-and-a-half with the Internal Revenue Service I felt I'd learned all I could from it," Bartolme said. "It became obvious that the Government can give you experience and security, but no wealth."

Bartolme, like Laurie Hancock, had obtained a salaried job that would give him the experience and teach him the techniques he'd need later to succeed in his own business. It's an effective technique and one that you, the reader, should consider in your own plans.

In looking for such a job to start your career that will lead to wealth, Bartolme believes you must do three things:

1. Become a part of a growth industry; that is, connect with a firm that is forging ahead in such fields as pollution and environmental control, electronics, chemicals, plastics, nuclear energy, and the like.

2. Seek out an expanding company, one that is known as a pace-setter in its field.

3. Check for progressive management, make certain the company you join has a management team known for its enlightened leadership, modern-thinking, and development of executive talent.

Once you've joined an expanding company in a growth industry, Bartolme advises, you should work by the job, not by the clock; ask intelligent questions of those above you so that you can learn as much as you can quickly about the business; and volunteer whenever possible for the odd assignment—particularly the one your associates shun.

These are the techniques that have worked for Ralph Bartolme; they'll also work for you. Try them.

Now at this point let me give you a caution against defeatism.

You've heard many people say: "It just isn't possible to make a fortune anymore with high taxes, inflation, government controls, and, furthermore, there aren't the opportunities there used to be."

Hogwash!

There are more opportunities today for the ambitious men and women than there've ever been in the history of the United States. People have more money to spend, they have more time in which to enjoy themselves, and they want new and innovative products, reacreational facilities, and whatever else money will buy to make their lives more enjoyable.

The men and women whose stories I've told in this book made most of their money in the 1960s. I predict the 1970s will offer even greater opportunities.

I personally have such confidence in the evergrowing economy of the United States that I've invested a good deal of my money in the common stocks of America's great corporations. I've done this through an investment counselor.

This is still another way to make your capital grow—invest it in stocks. I'm not recommending that you put all your money in stocks, only that you consider them as an investment for part of your wealth.

Finally, these are the five steps you must take to start yourself on your path to riches:

1. Begin this very moment, right now, to think of yourself as a success. Don't daydream that you're a success, but think of yourself as one in a practical sense. If you think of yourself as a success, you'll do and act as a successful man or woman—this will start your program of growth to riches.

2. Get a sheet of paper and list all the pluses and minuses—the positives and negatives—that can affect your pathway to riches. These items should include your education, your special knowledge, your experience, your finances, and every practical move that could be made either for or against your plan.

3. Now arrange the material you've collected into a sequence of progress. This means that what you have in mind—your goal—will have to follow from a logical sequence. So, list the steps you'll have to take to reach your goal.

4. Fix on your goal. Concentrate your interest on precisely what you want to accomplish. Do you strive for a better job, do you want to start a business of your own? Decide what your objective is and stick to it.

5. Now take two sheets of paper. Put a heading at the top of one, "Points That Favor the Achievement of My goal." And on the other put "Points Against the achievment of My Goal." This will enable you to decide

what obstacles you must overcome on your path to wealth as well as tell you what your attributes are that'll help you achieve it. Be honest in making these lists. Then keep them for constant reference. From time to time as you develop and move forward toward your goal you'll want to switch the items from one page to another. For instance, if one of the points against the achievement of your goal is lack of experience, you'll switch that later to a favorable point when you've gained the needed experience.

In the two years that I collected the material for this book, my eyes have been opened to the secrets the millionaires have used to amass their great wealth. And I discovered all their ideas, their plans, their decisions, and their devices are ones that anyone, who'll apply himself, can adopt and use.

I've recorded in this book all those ideas, plans, decisions and devices so that you can use them to achieve your own riches.

Now the choice is yours.

Never doubt that your dreams are within your reach. Our fast-paced world cries out for new ideas, and the men and women who work to transform ideas into reality are handsomely rewarded. You have it within your power to be one of these men or women.

But first you must believe it. You must grasp your destiny and never let it go. If you do you, too, will join the ranks of the winners—the place where you belong.

Good Luck.

Useful

Money-Making

Books

USEFUL MONEY-MAKING BOOKS

The books I've listed below can give you additional money-making ideas as well as serve ás a useful reference as you climb your ladder to success. Later, as you progress along your path to riches, you'll want to add books of your own selection to your reading list, but these will do as a start:

How to Start Your Own Business on a Shoestring and Make up to $100,000 per Year, by Tyler G. Hicks, $7.95, Parker Publishing Co., Inc., West Nyack, New York 10994.

The Successful Writer's Guide, by Hal D. Steward, $7.95, Parker Publishing Co., Inc., West Nyack, New York 10994.

Acquiring and Merging Businesses, by J. H. Hennessy, Jr., $19.95, Prentice-Hall, Inc., Englewood Cliffs, New Jersey 07632.

Tax Guide for Buying and Selling a Business, by Stanley Hagendorf, $19.95, Prentice-Hall, Inc., Englewood Cliffs, New Jersey 07632.

The Professional Job Hunting System, $14.95, Performance Dynamics, Verona, New Jersey 07044.

How to Think like a Millionaire and Get Rich, by Howard E. Hill, $6.95, Parker Publishing Co., Inc., West Nyack, New York 10994.

How to Build a Second-Income Fortune in Your Spare Time, by Tyler G. Hicks, $7.95, Parker Publishing Co., Inc., West Nyack, New York 10994

Smart Money Shortcuts to Becoming Rich, by Tyler G. Hicks, $7.95, Parker Publishing Co., Inc., West Nyack, New York 10994.